THE
ANCIENT
PERSIANS

Other titles in the *Lost Civilizations* series include:

LOST CIVILIZATIONS

THE ANCIENT PERSIANS

James Barter

LUCENT BOOKS

An imprint of Thomson Gale, a part of The Thomson Corporation

THOMSON

GALE

Detroit • New York • San Francisco • San Diego • New Haven, Conn. • Waterville, Maine • London • Munich

LIBRARY OF CONGRESS CATALOGING-IN-PUBLICATION DATA

Barter, James, 1946–
　　The ancient Persians / by James Barter
　　　　p. cm. — (Lost civilizations)
　　Includes bibliographical references and index.
　　ISBN 1-59018-621-4 (hardcover : alk. paper)
　　1. Iran—Civilization—To 640—Juvenile literature. I. Title. II. Series: Lost Civilizations.
DS267.B37 2005
935—dc22

2005013197

Printed in the United States of America

CONTENTS

FOREWORD

"What marvel is this?" asked the noted eighteenth-century German poet and philosopher Friedrich Schiller. "O earth . . . what is your lap sending forth? Is there life in the deeps as well? A race yet unknown hiding under the lava?" The "marvel" that excited Schiller was the discovery, in the early 1700s, of two entire ancient Roman cities buried beneath over 60 feet (18m) of hardened volcanic ash and lava near the modern city of Naples, on Italy's western coast. "Ancient Pompeii is found again!" Schiller joyfully exclaimed. "And the city of Hercules rises!"

People had known about the existence of long-lost civilizations before Schiller's day, of course. Stonehenge, a circle of huge, very ancient stones, had stood silent and mysterious, on a plain in Britain as long as people could remember. And the ruins of temples and other structures erected by the ancient inhabitants of Egypt, Palestine, Greece, and Rome had for untold centuries sprawled in magnificent profusion throughout the Mediterranean world. But when, why, and how were these monuments built? And what were the exact histories and beliefs of the peoples who built them? A few scattered surviving ancient literary texts had provided some partial answers to some of these questions. But not until Pompeii and Herculaneum started to emerge from the ashes did the modern world begin to study and re-construct lost civilizations in a systematic manner.

Even then, the process was at first slow and uncertain. Pompeii, a bustling, prosperous town of some twenty thousand inhabitants, and the smaller Herculaneum met their doom on August 24, A.D. 79, when the nearby volcano, Mt. Vesuvius, blew its top and literally erased them from the map. For nearly seventeen centuries their contents, preserved in a massive cocoon of volcanic debris, rested undisturbed. Not until the early eighteenth century did people begin raising statues and other artifacts from the buried cities; and at first this was done in a haphazard, unscientific manner. The diggers, who were seeking art treasures to adorn their gardens and mansions, gave no thought to the historical value of the finds. The sad fact was that at the time no trained experts existed to dig up and study lost civilizations in a proper manner.

This unfortunate situation began to change in 1763. In that year Johann J. Winckelmann, a German librarian fascinated by antiquities (the name then used for ancient artifacts), began to investigate Pompeii and Herculaneum. Although he made some mistakes and drew some wrong conclusions, Winckelmann laid the initial, crucial groundwork for a new science—archaeology (a term derived from two Greek words meaning "to talk about ancient things").

His book, *History of the Art of Antiquity*, became a model for the first generation of archaeologists to follow in their efforts to understand other lost civilizations. "With unerring sensitivity," noted scholar C.W. Ceram explains, "Winckelmann groped toward original insights, and expressed them with such power of language that the cultured European world was carried away by a wave of enthusiasm for the antique ideal. This . . . was of prime importance in shaping the course of archaeology in the following century. It demonstrated means of understanding ancient cultures through their artifacts."

In the two centuries that followed, archaeologists, historians, and other scholars began to piece together the remains of lost civilizations around the world. The glory that was Greece, the grandeur that was Rome, the cradles of human civilization in Egypt's Nile valley and Mesopotamia's Tigris-Euphrates valley, the colorful royal court of ancient China's Han Dynasty, the mysterious stone cities of the Maya and Aztecs in Central America—all of these

and many more were revealed in fascinating, often startling, if sometimes incomplete, detail by the romantic adventure of archaeological research. This work, which continues, is vital. "Digs are in progress all over the world," says Ceram. "For we need to understand the past five thousand years in order to master the next hundred years."

Each volume in the Lost Civilizations series examines the history, works, everyday life, and importance of ancient cultures. The archaeological discoveries and methods used to gather this knowledge are stressed throughout. Where possible, quotes by the ancients themselves, and also by later historians, archaeologists, and other experts, support and enliven the text. Primary and secondary sources are carefully documented by footnotes and each volume supplies the reader with an extensive Works Consulted list. These and other research tools afford the reader a thorough understanding of how a civilization that was long lost has once more seen the light of day and begun to reveal its secrets to its captivated modern descendants.

THE WORLD'S FIRST GREAT EMPIRE

Archaeological evidence reveals the presence of nomadic peoples in what would eventually be known as Persia as far back as 5000 B.C. and the existence of early villages about 3000 B.C. But it was not until another twenty-five hundred years or so had passed that the Persians rose to prominence.

In the year 550 B.C. the Persian people burst forth from obscurity to create a great empire. Within just two decades, a well-disciplined Persian military under the command of King Cyrus marched forth from what is today southwestern Iran to create a realm that dwarfed all others that had come before. And in merely two decades more, King Darius II further expanded Persia's boundaries to create an empire that encompassed 2.4 million square miles (6.2 million sq. km), most of what today is called the Middle East. From the Aegean coastline of modern Turkey east to the Indus River in northern India, and from the southern shores of the Black, Caspian, and Aral seas to the northern shores of the Persian Gulf and Red Sea, a series of Persian kings imposed their will upon dozens of smaller states and peoples. Contemporary historians such as A.T. Olmstead, author of *History of the Persian Empire*, recognize the significance of Darius II's achievement,

saying, "The Persian Empire was the world's first great Empire."[1] The Persian Empire's geographical scope was so immense that it would be unmatched until the height of Rome's power, some six hundred years later.

Ancient Persia's greatness was measured by more than mere size, however. In keeping with the majesty of their realm, kings constructed major metropolises strategically situated throughout the empire, built stately palaces to house noble families, and constructed temples to honor the Persian god known as Ahura Mazda, a name meaning "he who knows all." Some of Persian architecture surpassed in size and splendor many of the edifices built much later by the Greeks and Romans. And for their personal adornment, Persian kings commanded goldsmiths and other artisans to craft jewelry and works of art as intricate as any produced by craftsmen of other ancient civilizations. The Persians' success in holding together such an empire for more than two hundred years was not based on good fortune. It was the result of wise leaders who made it their job to assimilate a remarkable diversity of peoples, languages, and customs while respecting their differences and allowing their cultures to flourish.

Pictured here are ruins of a stairway and columns of King Darius's palace in Persepolis, the center of the Persian Empire.

An Empire Lost in Time

Yet despite the efforts of its rulers, the impressive wealth and success of the Persian Empire was eventually lost and forgotten. Not long after the empire's collapse in 330 B.C., little evidence of its existence remained. Although for hundreds of years visitors stopped to inspect the ruins of the cities the Persians had built, these artifacts offered little more than a glimpse into the empire's majestic past; those who looked upon these ruins could not possibly fully grasp Persia's onetime greatness. Palaces had long since collapsed or been burned to the ground by invaders; brightly colored frescoes and towering statuary had been sandblasted by hot, swirling desert winds; pottery and enameled artifacts lay scattered and broken. Even when found, treasures once buried deep beneath the shifting desert sands failed to provide visitors with a fair and accurate glimpse into the past of this once-vital empire. Olmstead notes that even scholars tended to undervalue the Persians accomplishments, asking, "Why should the Orientalist [historian who studies the Middle East] waste his time in shredding over the old straw [archaeological artifacts] when excavation after excavation in other more favored countries was every year pouring forth new treasures to astonish the world?"[2]

The written record left behind by Persians at the time fared little better than other works. One of the most remarkable oddities about Persian history is its lack of documentation by the Persians themselves. The Persian kings, unlike other leaders before or since, did not employ professional scribes to record the significant events of their reigns. Moreover, what records were kept were etched on clay tablets and stone statuary. Many of these records were either erased over centuries by blowing sands, were obliterated when they were dropped while being moved, or were used as construction material by later generations who failed to appreciate their significance.

As a consequence of this lack of records by the ancient Persians, for more than two millennia historians have depended upon the insights of Greeks who traveled in Persia and wrote about its culture. Ancient historians such as Herodotus, Xenophon, and Strabo provide insights into Persian kings, armies, and culture. Unfortunately for modern-day scholars, these chroniclers often suffered from an anti-Persian bias. Olmstead addresses the difficulties posed by Greek historians who presented an incomplete and sometimes distorted point of view, noting, "The majority of the available sources on Achaemenid [the Persian ruling dynasty] history were in Greek. . . . The natural consequence was that the history of the Achaemenid Empire was presented as a series of uncorrelated episodes which found unity and significance only when inserted into the story of the little Greek states."[3]

A Refreshing Turn of Events

Recently Persia's true achievements have come to light. Archaeologists have unearthed entire cities, stunningly beautiful artifacts, and ancient clay tablets bearing inscriptions that have brought Persia's rich history into sharp focus. For the first time, scholars and the general public are able to gain insights into an empire that within little more than two hundred years arose, matured, and faded away.

This new epoch in the discovery and understanding of the civilization that gave rise to the Persian Empire began in the early nineteenth century when archaeologists, primarily from America and Europe, conducted excavations at the sites of several historically significant Persian cities. These excavations in the desert yielded spectacular artifacts beyond scholars' imaginations. Palaces, stone statuary, clay tablets, painted pottery, and gold artifacts emerged to provide a picture of a sophisticated and mighty people. The historical accounts inscribed in clay, when evaluated alongside the works of Greek chroniclers of the time, add additional flavor, detail, and complexity to the knowledge of the time when the Persian Empire was the mightiest on Earth. For the first time in more than twenty-three hundred years, the ancient Persians have once again emerged to take their place among other great civilizations.

Chapter One

PERSIA BEFORE THE EMPIRE

Around 7500 B.C. during a time that anthropologists call the Early Neolithic, Persia was home to a scattering of nomadic tribes making their annual migrations. Leading the simplest of lives, they drove their herds of goats and sheep from grazing ground to grazing ground without any sense of permanency. But archaeologists say that in about 5000 B.C., the first settled civilizations arose. Archaeologists conducting excavations in many locations have unearthed troves of artifacts, such as the remains of rudimentary irrigation systems, clusters of simple but permanent structures, primitive metal tools, pottery, and graves showing evidence of ceremonial burials—all indicative of early settled civilizations. None of the peoples who created these settlements was known as a powerful or dominant civilization, however, and archaeologists are certain that this region was home to a mix of settled groups and nomadic tribes. It was the blend of these early settled peoples mixed with nomadic tribes that provided much of the foundation upon which the Persian Empire was built.

The Crossroads of Three Continents

Although these early civilizations were unique in a variety of ways, scholars agree that the most important factor in their development was geographical location. Geography has always played a role in the history of great civilizations, and those that once flourished in the Middle East are no exception. A look at a map shows that this region is situated at the intersection of three continents: Europe, Asia, and Africa. Geologists explain that hundreds of millions of years ago the region's key geographical features developed that would later play pivotal roles in determining where people settled.

A long depression in the earth's surface that slopes gradually downhill from the Black Sea to what is called today the Persian Gulf makes possible the flow of the Tigris and Euphrates rivers, which provided water for roughly 150,000 square miles (389,000 sq. km) of land. The result was a region where fertile soil, an abundance of water, and temperate climate made not just small settlements but also large cities possible. Of secondary importance were the Zagros Mountains that funneled additional water down to the rivers to their west.

As nascent civilizations began to flourish in the region, its geography made it a natural crossroads for nomadic tribes. As these early tribal peoples moved into the vast region, the first to arrive settled the most hospitable land situated between the Tigris and the Euphrates.

Early Life Between the Rivers

The 700-mile-wide (1,130km) swath of land through which the Tigris and Euphrates rivers flow to the Persian Gulf is called Mesopotamia, from the Greek word meaning "between the rivers." Each year these two rivers swelled and flooded with the winter snow melt from the Zagros Mountains. As the floodwaters receded, they would leave behind a thick layer of fertile silt, making this land some of the richest in the known world.

The southern end of Mesopotamia was particularly rich in natural resources. It was there that the first nomadic tribesmen ended their rootless lifestyle to settle in villages. They recognized that all of their needs could be met living off the abundance of fish, wildlife, fruits, and grazing livestock on the wild grasses. Although scholars know little about those first settlers, it seems plausible that the first villages developed as commercial centers where the various tribal peoples could sell their excess food crops and livestock or trade for items they otherwise could not produce for themselves.

As dozens of small villages sprang up, more was demanded of the rivers than merely providing water for crops. People relied on the rivers to wash clothes, quench their thirst, eliminate sewage, and float themselves and goods from village to village. Among these villages, one or two gradually developed into cities, dominating the region and forming primitive governments to control and regulate all the others. These early forms of government, always autocratic monarchies, marked some of the earliest experiments in which society was organized and regulated by a central authority.

Within a few hundred years of the arrival of the first settlers, Mesopotamia had seen the development of several major cities that

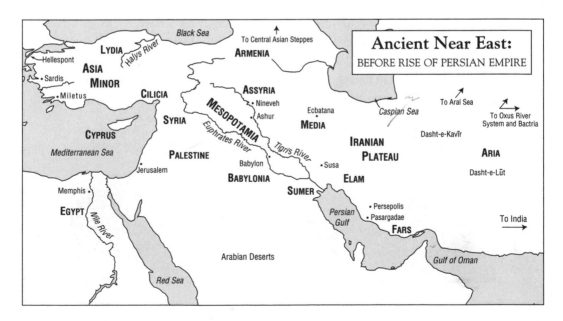

THE BEAUTY OF NINEVEH

Nineveh, the capital of ancient Assyria and one of the mightiest cities of all antiquity, was situated on the east bank of the Tigris River just opposite the site of the modern city of Mosul, Iraq. Until its excavation by Sir Austin Layard in the nineteenth century, it was scarcely known because its destruction at the hands of the Medes and the Babylonians was so extreme.

Fortunately, due to the efforts of Layard and others, the site of ancient Nineveh has been extensively excavated and its grandeur and architectural significance revealed. The city was enclosed by a rectangular wall roughly 3 miles (5km) long and 1.5 miles (2.4km) wide. It was so large that it is considered today to have been the first known metropolitan city with an estimated population of about fifty thousand. In the 1960s, the Iraq Department of Antiquities roofed the site over the palace of Sennacherib, one of only two preserved Assyrian palaces in the world, and began to allow visitors to tour it. The four restored rooms of the throne-room suite contain more than one hundred sculptures and beautifully decorated walls covered with colorful enamel tiles. In addition to the throne room, the palace contained two libraries (the contents of which were placed in the Louvre Museum in Paris and in the British Museum in London).

In addition to major architectural structures that have been excavated, such as the walls, the palace, and the libraries, archaeologists have found and restored hundreds of smaller artifacts that depict the daily lives of residents in the city more than four thousand years ago. Most significant are low-relief sculptures revealing traditional dress, hairstyles, temples, public gardens, animals wandering the streets, and figurines of religious significance.

An artist's rendering based on historical records tries to capture the glory that was ancient Nineveh.

left their cultural mark on the region. Of these, none were more highly developed than Nineveh and Babylon.

Majestic Cities of Incomparable Beauty

These two cities were the earliest of what scholars term metropolitan centers. Archaeologists excavating Nineveh and Babylon have unearthed evidence of large complexes of buildings, defensive walls surrounding each city, beautifully painted bricks depicting life in the cities, lush public parks, elaborate palaces for the kings, and stone-paved streets.

The first of the great cities of Mesopotamia, Nineveh was enclosed by a fortification wall 7 miles (11km) in perimeter. Built of rectangular stone blocks stacked without mortar, the wall was interrupted by four main gates with wooden doors. At the center of the city were temples, the king's palace, and large public parks, all accessed by broad, stone-paved roads passable in any weather. Excavations during the twentieth century revealed an aqueduct running from a nearby lake that supplied the city with clean drinking water and a reservoir for water storage during hot, dry summers.

The one city in ancient Mesopotamia of greater renown than Nineveh was Babylon. Herodotus, who actually traveled to Babylon, described it as standing upon a spacious plain, surrounded by a wall 56 miles (90km) long and wide enough to accommodate a four-horse chariot along the top. The city had eight entry gates, one of which, the Ishtar Gate, stood 47 feet (14m) tall and 32 feet (9.8m) wide and was covered in colorful painted tiles. This manner of decoration, Herodotus reported, was to serve as a beacon to attract the attention of distant travelers.

Babylon was known throughout the ancient world as a place of remarkable beauty. Through its center flowed the Euphrates River, busy with cargo and fishing boats as well as bathers. Excavations have revealed that most of the buildings in Babylon were brick and were covered with enameled tiles of blue, yellow, or white, which were adorned with animal and other figures. The most prominent edifice in Babylon was the ziggurat, a huge series of stepped structures one stacked atop the next, rising in seven stages of gleaming enamel 650 feet (198m) into the air. On top of the ziggurat was the holiest of temples.

Perhaps most famous of all the wonders of Babylon were its hanging gardens. According to ancient literary texts, King Nebuchadnezzar built them on top of his palace for one of his wives to keep her cool and happy during the hot summers. The topmost terrace was covered with rich soil where a variety of flowers and large trees were planted. Hydraulic machines manned by slaves watered the plants 75 feet (23m) above the ground. In this way, in the cool shade of trees and surrounded by fragrant flowers, the women of the royal court walked, shielded from the view of commoners passing far below.

Cultural Advances

The growth of major cities was impressive but not as impressive as the cultural advances taking place within their confines. As metropolitan centers grew, the best minds were attracted to them, providing ideas and inventions so impressive that many are still in use today. Around 3000 B.C. in the cities of Ur and Uruk, which were part of the southern Mesopotamian kingdom known as Sumer, thinkers began to investigate their world in a way other Mesopotamian peoples did not. Historians do not yet understand this difference. Within five hundred years, however, the Sumerians developed disciplines such as science and mathematics, the first law code, and unprecedented artistry in working with gold, silver, and ceramics.

Notable for its importance to trade and commerce was the Sumerians' appreciation of the importance of mathematics. Traders and merchants, desperate to keep accurate accounts of inventories, learned to count by base ten; add, subtract, multiply, and divide; and even to understand the basic concept of fractions for calculating the contents of containers only partially filled. Accounts were entered onto clay tablets, and merchants "signed" them by rolling a small cylinder over the still-damp clay, leaving behind an embossed design unique to that merchant. As their sophistication in the manipulation of numbers increased, the Sumerians discovered the concepts of squares and cubes, and then of square and cube roots.

Mathematicians applied the idea of squares by helping farmers in calculating the size of their fields. As mathematicians applied their insights, they discovered the geometric principles of squares, rectangles, triangles, and circles. They further discovered the importance of angles and were the first to divide a circle into 360 degrees and then to define a right angle as comprising 90 degrees. Thanks to Sumerian discoveries in geometry, farmers were able to mark their fields accurately and build straight roads that ran between parcels of land, thereby maximizing the use of land. The concept of cubes and their roots was of similar impor-

tance in measuring volume. This mathematical advance was useful to merchants and their customers since now everyone would have a way of knowing how much of a product they were selling and buying. For example, a merchant could accurately measure the amount of grain he was selling, and his customer could know for certain that he was receiving the amount of grain promised for the agreed upon price.

Moreover, measures were standardized. An example of a standardized measure is the "royal cubit" found by archaeologists. It is a black limestone ruler, exactly 18 inches (46cm) in length, and is inscribed with a name—presumably the ruler's owner. Including the owner's name, scholars speculate, meant that someone could be held accountable for the accuracy of a measurement.

Sumerian practicality also showed in the way inventors watched farmers and craftsmen hard at work and imagined ways to ease their labor while increasing productivity. For example, early inventors recognized that the thousands of clay pots used to store cooking oils, grains, and other small items could be made faster by forming them on a spinning wheel remarkably similar to those used by modern potters. Archaeologists who have unearthed primitive stone potter's wheels in the ruins of the city of Uruk call them the first real mechanical device ever invented. Sumerian inventors watched early farmers breaking up the land with their hands and feet and saw the need for simple hoes and picks. These tools consisted of a blade of bronze—a metal made from combining tin with copper—connected to a wooden handle. Other innovators stood on the banks of the Tigris and Euphrates rivers as rowers struggled to propel boats up and

This clay tablet, more than four thousand years old, records in cuneiform text the surface area of a plot of land in Mesopotamia.

down the waterways and hit on the idea of a single sail connected to a mast to harness the wind to boat effortlessly.

Still other Sumerians stared at the night sky and eventually realized that certain objects, such as planets, were appearing and disappearing in a regular pattern in the course of a year. Based on the constantly changing positions of the planets, they were the first to understand that the seasons recurred predictably and advised farmers on when to plant their crops. These ancient astronomers were the first to understand that these cosmic motions define the year; they subdivided the year into months and eventually into 360 days. They later even subdivided the day into 24 hours.

None of these discoveries and innovations made by the Sumerians would have impacted all of Mesopotamia and later the Persian Empire had not some way of recording them been invented. For this reason,

virtually all historians acknowledge that the one Sumerian invention that stands above all others was their written language, called cuneiform. This system of writing used pictures that could either represent objects directly or express a sound similar to the spoken word for an object. Such a system made it possible to make a permanent record of abstract concepts.

The Aryan Incursions

While the peoples of Mesopotamia were thriving in their lush river environment, unbeknownst to them, incursions were taking place in the lands to the east by tribes of nomadic peoples known to historians as Aryans. These tribal peoples, some of whom would later be known as Persians, began moving in waves into what is today Iran between 2000 B.C. and 1600 B.C. Historians speculate that the Aryans were fleeing the harsh climate around the Caspian Sea, where wintertime temperatures rarely rose above freezing but where summertime temperatures often exceeded 90° F (32° C).

The archaeological record indicates that as the Aryan tribes traveled south, some turned east. Around the year 800 B.C., two of those tribes, the Medes and the Persians, settled along the eastern shoulder of the Zagros Mountains that separated them from Mesopotamia. The Medes settled toward

CUNEIFORM

Historians and sociologists studying civilizations are in general agreement that the most significant characteristic of each civilization is its unique language. They are also in agreement that the first written language was invented in about 3000 B.C. when unknown scribes began using cuneiform, whose name is derived from the Latin word *cuneus*, meaning "wedge."

Archaeologists excavating in the city of Uruk during the nineteenth century uncovered piles of clay tablets bearing what appeared to be some form of primitive writing using combinations of wedge shapes and straight lines. Epigraphists, archaeologists specializing in the study of inscriptions, are certain that the first use of cuneiform was to record trading transactions such as the number of goats traded for some amount of wheat, directions to a marketplace, or the amount of grain a ship could carry. Gradually, however, cuneiform was used to document laws, history, and significant cultural events.

Scribes first developed the cuneiform style by scratching pictures into wet clay with a reed or a stick. As the language evolved and became phonetically based, scribes developed a combination of six hundred triangular wedge-shaped forms combined with straight lines, each representing a phonetic sound. To press the wedge shape into the clay, they used a stylus, a straight piece of reed with a three-cornered end.

Cuneiform is the oldest known written language. Scribes imprinted the characters on wet clay using a reed.

the northern end of the mountain range and the Persians toward the southern end.

The lands where the Medes and the Persians settled were far less hospitable than Mesopotamia, which was already heavily populated and where peoples there were too well-organized militarily to force out. Left with lands that could not support permanent settlements, the newcomer tribes were forced to continue their nomadic migrations in sparse, hilly terrain offering little vegetation during the hot summer and little protection from the winds during the brutally cold winter. Although their new living conditions were difficult, they were still an improvement over what they had experienced near the Caspian Sea.

Nomadic Life

The Persians and their fellow nomads made use of long-known survival techniques as they and their herds of goats and sheep made their annual nomadic migrations. For example, a wide, gravelly wash, despite being dry in the summer, was a place where water might be found by digging deep holes, and the prickly buds of scrubby plants called euphorbs could be plucked of their sharp needles and eaten. Loading their carts each morning following a breakfast of unleavened bread, a piece of lamb, and goat milk, these hearty nomads constantly remained on the move. Young adults watched the animals as they grazed, the men hunted small mammals and birds, and the women foraged for edible plants.

Nomadic life could at times be violent. Without clearly defined boundaries, tribes occasionally wandered into territory claimed by other tribes. The perpetual shortage of food and water made tribes apt to jealously guard lands they considered theirs. This situation became more acute over the course of centuries as more and more northern tribes found their way south into the Iranian plateau. From the standpoint of the Aryan nomads, there was only one direction they could go to improve their conditions, and that was over the Zagros Mountains to the west, into the already-settled lands of Mesopotamia.

A Region in Turmoil

Sometime between 700 B.C. and 650 B.C., the peoples of the city-states within Mesopotamia became aware of the threat posed by the wanderers. The one power within Mesopotamia willing to challenge the interlopers was Assyria, in the northern stretch of the river valley. The Assyrians had recently gained power by attacking and subjugating the Babylonians to the south. Now dominating a broad stretch of Mesopotamia, they were particularly troubled by the Medes, who occupied the northeastern slope of the mountain range. Following a hundred years of relative peace, relations between the peoples on either side of the Zagros were on the verge of boiling over into a full-scale war.

Assyria mounted two campaigns to destroy the Medes but without achieving a decisive victory. Clashes between the two only strengthened the resolve of the Medes, who drew support from an increasing number of other nomadic tribes east of the Zagros. The Medes also proved to be superior fighters. Mede rulers, especially Cyaxares II, arrayed their soldiers in battle with greater effectiveness than the Assyrians did. Ready to take his army into a pitched battle against the Assyrians, he first approached the Babylonian

In the sixth century B.C., *Persian ruler Cyrus the Great conquered the powerful Medes, a victory that marked the beginning of the rise of Persia as a military power.*

king Nabopolassar for assistance against their common enemy. In about 614 B.C. the combined armies of the Medes and the Babylonians invaded Assyria and crushed its king and army.

The turmoil had just begun. Not content with the destruction of Assyria, and bent on establishing an empire, Cyaxares conquered other smaller nations to his north. His conquests took him up to the Caspian Sea and then west into what today is Turkey before he died in 584 B.C. Following Cyaxares'

death came a thirty-year period of relative peace as a result of clever diplomacy among the region's kings.

The Persians living along the southeastern slope of the Zagros range were one of the Aryan cultures that avoided conflict with the Medes yet were forced to acknowledge their dominance. Although both the Medes and the Persians were descended from the earlier Aryan immigrants, there was a festering sense of mistrust between the two, especially as each grew in power.

The Rise of Persia and Entrance of Cyrus the Great

At the beginning of the sixth century B.C., when the authority of the Medes was ascending, the Persians were largely unknown throughout the region known today as the Middle East. The Aryan nomads of the southern Zagros Mountains had long since ceased their wandering to settle into a region called Fars. The name of this region gradually changed to Pars, and later the Greeks called it Persia. Persians spent difficult lives scratching out an existence in dry, rocky soil far from a steady source of water. According to historian George Grote:

> The native Persians were an aggregate of seven agricultural, and four nomadic, tribes—all of them rude, hardy, and brave—dwelling in a mountainous region, clothed in skins, ignorant of wine, or fruit, or any of the commonest luxuries of life, and despising the very idea of purchase or sale.[4]

It was in this rugged region that Persia's first great king was born. The ruling family of Persia, the Achaemenids, had cowered before the might of the Medes during the rule of Cyaxares. However, sometime between 590 B.C. and 580 B.C. a boy was born who would one day bring an end to the Mede dominance.

The birth, boyhood, and rise to power of this child, named Cyrus, is imperfectly known. Modern historians seeking information on Cyrus have little to choose from in the way of sources. Both of the ancient Greek chroniclers, Herodotus and Xenophon, tell

In this drawing, King Cyaxares II (on horseback) addresses Mede soldiers before going into battle. The Medes were the dominant power in the Middle East before the Persians.

differing stories about his early years. Moreover, most accounts are largely fanciful legends borrowed from mythology. Herodotus, for example, recorded that the baby Cyrus had been left to die on a mountaintop but that a shepherd found him and raised him. Later, the boy demonstrated leadership qualities and courage that could only be found in someone of noble birth. Since this is the same story associated with the mythi-

THE HAMMURABI LAW CODE

Law codes are found in every modern nation. Although all of these codes have some laws in common, they also include laws that are unique to each nation. For centuries, law scholars had speculated on the origin of the first law code and what laws it might contain. In 1901 archaeologists excavating the Persian city of Susa were able to answer those two questions.

Workers clearing rubble uncovered a black stone measuring about 9 by 4 feet (3 by 1.25 m) and inscribed with row after row of cuneiform text and a low-relief sculpture of King Hammurabi receiving the laws from the god known as Shamash. Based on the identification of Hammurabi, historians dated the stone to around 1740 B.C. and believed it was originally placed for public view in a temple in Babylon. On this stone, translators discovered 282 laws inscribed.

The code covers mainly four categories: economical considerations, family matters, crime, and civil matters. The law code is quite detailed, and it even contains recommendations on reasonable rates for services and trade. The basis of the criminal law expresses the notion of "an eye for an eye," meaning that an injured party is entitled to equal retaliation against the party that caused the injury. Many offenses could be compensated for with money.

This stone stele features King Hammurabi's law code, inscribed in rows and rows of cuneiform text.

cal Greek king Oedipus, modern scholars tend to discount Herodotus's narrative. The one historian who provided a fairly plausible account was Diodorus Siculus, who noted that Cyrus was actually part Median since he was the grandson of the Median king Astyages:

> Cyrus, the son of Cambyses and Mandane, the daughter of Astyages who was king of the Medes, was pre-eminent among the men of his time in bravery and sagacity and the other virtues; for his father had reared him after the manner of kings and had made him zealous to emulate the highest achievements. And it was clear that he would take hold of great affairs, since he revealed an excellence beyond his years.[5]

One cuneiform tablet excavated in 1879 and dating to 538 B.C. states that Cyrus was descended from a long line of royalty: "I am Cyrus, king of the world, great king, mighty king, . . . son of Cambyses, great king, king of Anshan, grandson of Cyrus, great king, king of Anshan, descendant of Teispes, great king, king of Anshan, progeny of an unending royal line."[6]

The little that is known of Cyrus's childhood suggests that he had a commanding personality but was raised, despite his royal lineage, in poverty compared to the lifestyles of the Medes or other peoples of Mesopotamia. At some time, probably about 560 B.C., he rose to power and assumed the kingship of all the Persians. Despising the Medes even though he was related to them, Cyrus soon mobilized an army of rugged citizen soldiers against them. The rise of Persia had begun.

CHAPTER TWO

MASTERS OF THE PERSIAN EMPIRE

As one foe after another fell, Persian dominance spread from the Zagros Mountains west to the Aegean Sea. Persia's armies implemented well-conceived strategies to vanquish their enemies while kings mastered the diplomacy necessary for creating a flourishing culture and maintaining peace in the conquered lands. Within the span of only seventy years, the first four in a line of Persian kings expanded the empire to its zenith and administered it so successfully that for ages to come kings would study their methods and try to apply them to their own realms.

Treason Hands Cyrus
His First Victory

Fifth-century B.C. historians say that Cyrus understood that a victory over the Medes could not be accomplished by simply marching against their capital city, Ecbatana. The Median army was well trained and filled with veteran soldiers while the Persian army was largely unskilled and without battle experience. To overcome this disadvantage, Cyrus employed a clever strategy. He determined whether he could detect any resentment towards King Astyages among Median noble families that might motivate them to join him. As Astyages' grandson, Cyrus was in a good position to make this assessment.

Cyrus learned that discontent toward Astyages was rife. Astyages' style of rule was ruthless and created resentment among conquered tribes and even among some of the Median nobility. Subject nations had been forced to contribute burdensome taxes as well as fighting men to serve the king. Cyrus secretly made overtures to several noble Median families and promised that if they would support him in a war against Astyages, in return he would treat them as equals to Persians rather than as vanquished foes. Cyrus then turned to the Babylonian king, Nabonidus, with a similar offer in exchange for his support.

Astyages, now growing aware that his grandson might be plotting against him, yet unaware that many of his own people had pledged their allegiance to Cyrus, summoned the Median army to prepare for war. Herodotus tells the story of the battle:

> So when the two armies met and engaged, only a few of the Medes, who were not in on the secret, fought; others deserted openly to the Persians; while the greater number counterfeited fear, and fled. Astyages, on learning of the shameful flight and dispersion of his army, broke out into

threats against Cyrus, saying, "Cyrus shall nevertheless have no reason to rejoice"; . . . he [Astyages] armed all the Medes who had remained in the city, both young and old; and leading them against the Persians, fought a battle, in which he was utterly defeated.[7]

In this way, in 550 B.C. the first of many battles involving armies of the Persian Empire took place. True to his word, Cyrus rewarded all who supported him in battle and even entered Ecbatana displaying compassion and forgiveness toward those who had fought against him. With this gesture, Cyrus earned a reputation as a just and honorable conqueror, a reputation that would pay him future dividends.

Cyrus's first success merely whetted his appetite for more. Within one year of his

conquest of the Medians, he was again on the march. The battles to come would prove that he was not just a clever strategist but a skilled and intrepid warrior as well.

Brilliant Strategies Crush the Lydian Kingdom

Cyrus next set out to conquer the kingdom to the west of Media, known as Lydia. On the western border of Media flowed the 700-mile-long (1130km) Halys River. This river, which averages about 75 feet (23m) wide and flows north into the Black Sea, formed a formidable boundary between the kingdoms of the Medes and the Lydians. Cyrus, however, was filled with confidence that he could cross the Halys and capture Lydia.

The leader of this rich and powerful nation, King Croesus, was reputed to be the wealthiest man on earth. Cyrus reckoned

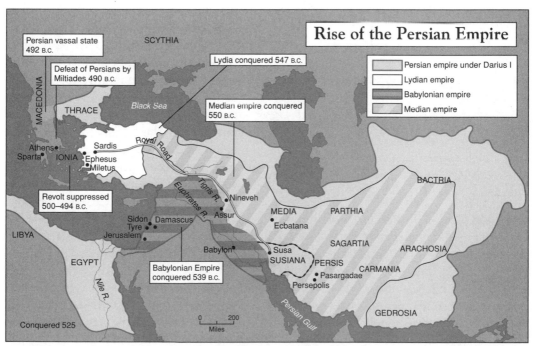

Rise of the Persian Empire

Persian vassal state 492 B.C.

SCYTHIA

Lydia conquered 547 B.C.

Defeat of Persians by Miltiades 490 B.C.

	Persian empire under Darius I
	Lydian empire
	Babylonian empire
	Median empire

MACEDONIA

THRACE

Black Sea

Median empire conquered 550 B.C.

Athens
Sparta
IONIA
Sardis
Ephesus
Miletus

Royal Road

BACTRIA

Revolt suppressed 500–494 B.C.

Euphrates R.
Tigris R.
Nineveh

Assur

MEDIA
Ecbatana

PARTHIA

Sidon
Tyre
Damascus
Jerusalem

LIBYA

Babylon

Susa
SUSIANA
PERSIS

SAGARTIA

ARACHOSIA

CARMANIA

EGYPT

Babylonian Empire conquered 539 B.C.

Pasargadae
Persepolis

Nile R.

Conquered 525

0   200
Miles

Persian Gulf

GEDROSIA

This drawing depicts the wealthy Lydian king Croesus being brought before his conqueror, Cyrus of Persia.

Herodotus informs his readers that to be certain that he would be victorious, the cautious and superstitious Croesus sent a delegation to consult the oracle at the Greek city of Delphi since she claimed to have the power to predict future events. The oracle, who was a priestess of the god Apollo, invited the Lydian delegation to be seated and to ask their question. One delegate asked whether Croesus should go to war with the Persians. The oracle responded that if Croesus crossed the Halys and attacked the Persians, he would destroy a mighty empire.

The delegation returned to report the prophecy to Croesus. Delighted with what he interpreted to be the prediction of a military success over the Persians, Croesus readied his army for war. In 547 B.C. Croesus forded the Halys, capturing the Median fortress of Pteria before Cyrus could field his army. There, Croesus confidently awaited the arrival of the Persian army that he was certain he would destroy. Two months later, in 546 B.C., Cyrus arrived with his army, and a bloody daylong battle ensued. Thousands of archers, foot soldiers, and mounted horsemen shot, slashed, and trampled each other until nightfall, when both armies withdrew, still uncertain of the outcome. Croesus, cautious and believing he was at a disadvantage because he was outnumbered, retreated to Sardis, his capital city, hoping that Cyrus would not follow. Cyrus, however, had other intentions. Herodotus tells his readers that Cyrus pursued Croesus so quickly that "he was himself the first to announce his coming to the Lydian king."[8]

that conquering Lydia and eliminating Croesus would elevate Persia to the status of the most powerful and feared kingdom in the world and himself to a position from which he could rule the world. Croesus, however, had similar designs about crossing the Halys to capture some of the territory Cyrus had just seized.

Croesus collected his army on the broad plains in front of Sardis, placed his best mounted warriors in the middle, and prepared for the final battle that he still believed would "destroy a mighty empire." But Cyrus, ever the brilliant strategist, had an unpleasant surprise in store for Croesus. Cyrus, knowing from experience that horses would stampede at the smell of camels, ordered his generals to bring forward all the camels that his army had been using as pack animals. Herodotus relates what came next: "The two armies then joined battle, and immediately the Lydian war-horses, seeing and smelling the camels, turned round and galloped off; and so it came to pass that all Croesus' hopes withered away."[9]

The victory over the Lydians sent a shock wave throughout the region. Cyrus had doubled the extent of the Persian Empire, had brought untold wealth to the Persian people, and had proven the Persian army a seemingly invincible force.

The Destruction of the Babylonians

In 540 B.C., following seven years needed to organize his new empire, Cyrus launched an attack against the last remaining obstacle to his undisputed dominance of the Middle East, the kingdom of Babylonia, which he conquered in 539 B.C.. Just as had been the case with his attacks against the Medes and the Lydians, this one involved another clever ruse that demonstrated why Cyrus was now becoming known as "Cyrus the Great."

Babylon had been partially protected by the Gyndes River, a daunting tributary of the Tigris. Rapids in parts of the river were so swift and dangerous that Cyrus knew that his army could not cross safely. Not to be de-

terred, Cyrus set out to alter the river's course in order for his troops to cross. He divided his army into 180 units and ordered each unit to dig a shallow channel that would drain water away from the river to lessen its force. Cyrus's army then safely crossed, entered Babylonia, and in the battle that ensued destroyed the Babylonian army.

The Persian nobility had become emboldened by their leader's success and suggested to Cyrus that it might be an opportune time for them to move out of their poor and desolate lands for the far more fertile and lush lands to the west. Herodotus reports Cyrus's answer to their suggestion, which reveals the king's toughness: "Do so if you wish, but if you do, be ready to find yourselves no longer governors but governed; for soft lands breed soft men; it does not happen that the same land brings forth wonderful crops and good fighting men."[10] Cyrus's success only motivated him to undertake further conquest. Yet, as is often the case, warriors grow old, they encounter a more formidable adversary, or their luck simply runs out. Such was the case with Cyrus. In 530 B.C., during a small engagement against a minor enemy, Cyrus was killed by an enemy archer's arrow. The body of Persia's first emperor was returned to the royal city of Pasargadae, where it was placed in a simple tomb. Yet Persia's expansion was not yet at an end.

By the time he died in 530 B.C., Cyrus had delivered all of what today is called the Middle East to his peoples. The lone exception was Egypt. The Greek warrior and historian Xenophon leaves little doubt about the empire's immense size and the number of different cultures brought within the scope of Persian dominance:

He [Cyrus] ruled over these nations, even though they did not speak the same language as he, nor one nation the same as another. Moreover, the tribes that he brought into subjection to himself were so many that it is a difficult matter even to travel to them all, in whatever direction one begins one's journey from the palace, whether toward the east or the west, toward the north or the south.[11]

Following Cyrus's burial, his will was read. In it, Cyrus gave directions for his el-dest son, Cambyses II, to become king. Following the coronation, Cambyses set his sights on the one great realm that remained to be conquered, Egypt.

Cambyses Takes Egypt

Of all the lands in the ancient Middle East, none was more admired for its long and rich cultural history than Egypt. Much like the Sumerians, the Egyptians had a reputation for cultural riches. Egyptian thinkers were revered for their advances in astronomy, mathematics, engineering, and language. Adding Egypt to Persia's empire would be the

The victorious Cyrus enters the gates of Babylon in 539 B.C. The Persian leader's conquest of the great Mesopotamian city established him as the undisputed ruler of the Middle East.

Cambyses II mounts his horse and flees from an Egyptian temple after slaughtering a bull that was sacred to the priests.

crowning achievement of his reign, and Cambyses II wasted no time leading his troops south to the land along the Nile River.

Before Cyrus died, he had tasked Cambyses with the initial planning for an invasion of Egypt. Herodotus explains that in keeping with Cyrus's tradition of entering each nation with a well-conceived battle plan, Cambyses and his army entered Egypt where the Egyptians would least expect them: from across the Sinai desert. The Egyptian general Phanes deserted to Cambyses and advised him to hire nomads living in the desert as guides. As Herodotus tells the story, Phanes paid a great price for his treachery. He had left his two sons behind in Egypt, thinking that his betrayal would not be discovered, but as the armies of the Persians and the Egyptians met, his sons were brought out in front of the Egyptian army where they could be seen by their father. There, in full view, their throats were slit over a large bowl and their blood was mixed with water and wine before being drunk by some of the Egyptian army. Such a ghoulish display, however, did not dishearten the Persians, who overcame their foe.

Cambyses, however, did not possess his father's sense of compassion in dealing with the vanquished foe nor had he an appreciation for their culture. He angered all Egyptians by capturing their king, Psamtek III, and sending him off to Susa, in Persia, in chains. He further outraged the Egyptians by showing disregard for their religious convictions by driving his dagger into the neck of a bull that the Egyptians believed to be sacred. He also deliberately burned the embalmed mummy of Psamtek's father, King Amasis. Herodotus also reports the looting of temples by Persian troops.

Such disrespectful behavior on the part of Cambyses aroused anger and resentment among the Egyptians that would last for several generations. They never accepted Persian dominance and were continually inciting revolts against Persian governors. Cambyses did not live to see much of Egypt's defiance. In 522 B.C. he was assassinated by someone claiming to be his younger brother. Whoever this imposter was, he was not tolerated for long. Seven months later, he was assassinated by Persian nobles who replaced him with Darius, a legitimate member of the Achaemenid family.

Darius Calms the Empire and Sets His Sights on Europe

Coming off the difficult nine years that followed the death of Cyrus, the Persian people welcomed Darius. The new king immediately set himself to the task of reversing the results of some of Cambyses' ill-considered actions and recapturing the majesty of the empire built by Cyrus.

Darius's first task was to bring calm to the empire, which was reeling from a series of uprisings triggered by Cambyses' assassination. These uprisings were spontaneous and uncoordinated, and Darius and his generals were able to suppress them one by one. Such a succession of military engagements was a risky undertaking since Darius had at his disposal only a relatively small army. As historian A.R. Burn points out, "Darius and his friends fought nineteen battles and killed or led captive nine kings. One marvels at first sight that either he or the unity of the empire survived."[12]

Darius had no intentions of achieving less than his predecessors. In keeping with the precedent set during Cyrus's extraordinary rule, Darius wanted to expand the empire. With that in mind, he turned his gaze toward Europe. In 512 B.C. Darius led an army across the Hellespont (today called the Dardanelles), the 1-mile-wide (1.6km) strait connecting the Aegean with the Black Sea, and laid siege to several cities in Thrace and Macedonia, north of Greece.

Most distressed by Darius's uncontested invasion of the European mainland were the Greeks. Not one united country, Greece was a collection of dozens of independent city-states, each with a different and sometimes conflicting view of how to resist the Persian threat. Darius believed that the Greeks, without a common leader, would be unable to resist his army. What Darius had not considered, however, was the close alliance each city-state had with all the others. Although each city-state was independent, all were bound by a common language, history, and religion. It was this cultural bond that caused Darius problems. In 498 B.C., while he was threatening Greece, a group of city-states located along the Ionian coast in what today is

Turkey, revolted against him. These city-states were Greek, and they asked for help from Athens. Together, Athenian and Ionian soldiers marched on the Persian city Sardis and burned it to the ground.

When Darius heard of the destruction of Sardis, he swore to take revenge. Herodotus reported with great drama the Persian king's response upon hearing the news:

King Darius received tidings of the taking and burning of Sardis by the Athenians and Ionians. . . . He asked who the Athenians were, and being

This low-relief sculpture depicts King Darius I, who brought peace to the empire after Cambyses was assassinated in 522 B.C.

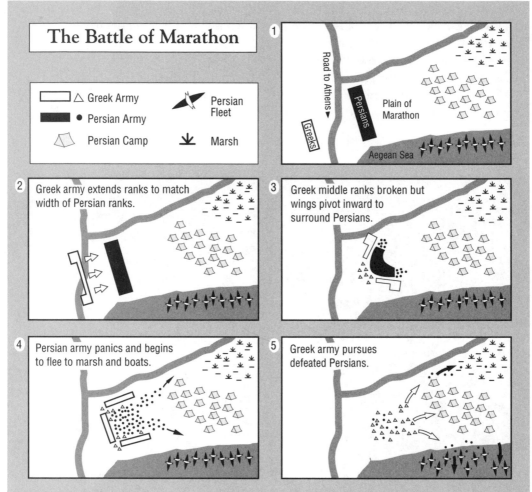

The Battle of Marathon

Legend:
- ▢ △ Greek Army
- ▬ ● Persian Army
- ⛺ Persian Camp
- Persian Fleet
- ↓ Marsh

1 Road to Athens ▼ | Greeks | Persians | Plain of Marathon | Aegean Sea

2 Greek army extends ranks to match width of Persian ranks.

3 Greek middle ranks broken but wings pivot inward to surround Persians.

4 Persian army panics and begins to flee to marsh and boats.

5 Greek army pursues defeated Persians.

At the Battle of Marathon in 490 B.C., the Greeks defeated the Persians with a clever military strategy.

informed, asked for his bow, and placing an arrow on the string, shot upward into the sky, saying as he let the shaft fly, "Grant me Zeus, to revenge myself on the Athenians!" After this speech, he bade one of his servants every day, when his dinner was spread, three times repeat these words to him—"Master, remember the Athenians."[13]

Darius Invades Greece

Darius immediately made plans to invade the Greek mainland. Military preparations for the invasion took several years. In 493 B.C., following several years of preparation, Darius gathered a large fleet of six hundred ships along with his army and invaded Greece from the north. But when the fleet approached a peninsula where Mount Athos looms high above the landscape, a treacherous storm swept across the cape, destroying three hundred ships and forcing Darius to retreat and rebuild his fleet.

In 491 B.C. Darius loaded his army onboard a new fleet under the command of two generals, Artaphernes and Datis, and sent them directly across the Aegean, island hopping, until they arrived on the Greek mainland at the large coastal plain of Marathon in 490 B.C.. The Persians' plan was to land there, march to Athens just 26 miles (42km) to the south, and burn the city to the ground.

For all of the time he had spent preparing militarily for the invasion, Darius had neglected to gain a true understanding of his enemy. As a consequence, Darius had underestimated the resolve of the Greeks and their ability to unite against a common foe. To the surprise of Artaphernes and Datis, as

they mustered their troops to march south, they were blocked along the western side of Marathon by soldiers from Athens and a few other city-states in central Greece. As the battle began, the Greek army also employed a tactic that the Persians had not anticipated. Herodotus describes the stratagem that won the Battle of Marathon:

> So when the battle was set in array . . . instantly the Athenians . . . charged the barbarians [Persians] at a run. The Persians, therefore, when they saw the Greeks coming on at speed, made ready to receive them, although it seemed to them that the Athenians were bereft of their senses, and bent upon their own destruction. . . . But the Athenians in close array fell upon them, and fought in a manner worthy of being recorded. They were the first of the Greeks, so far as I know, who introduced the custom of charging the enemy at a run.[14]

The Persian army, larger but not as well trained or as disciplined as the Greek army, was driven back to its boats pursued all the way by the Greeks. How bad a rout the Persians suffered is still being questioned by scholars. Herodotus reported the casualties on the Persian side as being 6,400 while the Greeks suffered a mere 192 killed, but modern historians find such a lopsided result implausible and suspect that Herodotus, who was himself Greek, was displaying bias in his report.

Whatever the casualty figures might have been, the outcome of the Battle of Marathon was celebrated by the Greeks as a major victory. To the Persians, however, the defeat was a minor setback. As soon as Darius received news of the defeat, he vowed to return with a better invasion plan, as Herodotus tells his readers: "Now when tidings of the battle that had been fought at Marathon reached the ears of King Darius, . . . his anger against the Athenians, . . . waxed still fiercer, and he became more than ever eager to lead an army against Greece."[15] Darius, however, never got another opportunity to exact revenge on Athens. He died in 486 B.C., not long after naming his son Xerxes to succeed him. Xerxes, as was the case with all of his predecessors, hoped to leave a legacy of expansion for the empire, and Greece remained the prime target.

Xerxes Invades Greece

When Xerxes took power, his future, and that of the Persian Empire, seemed limitless. In keeping with the tradition of his predecessors, Xerxes made careful preparations for his invasion of Greece. Years before the invasion date, he sent heralds to strike treaties of friendship with many city-states to allow his troops safe passage and to provision them. He also ordered his engineers to build needed bridges. The Persian king left nothing to chance—even ordering his men to dig a channel through the peninsula near Mount Athos to avoid losing the fleet as had happened in 493 B.C.

In 480 B.C. Xerxes made his move. His first objective was to transport his army across the Hellespont. To accomplish this feat, his engineers lashed six hundred warships together side by side to function as a temporary floating bridge. When the army had safely crossed, Xerxes ordered the warships to sail south safely through the canal that his men had earlier dug at Mount Athos.

The invasion went as planned for both the army and fleet until the army came to a pass at Thermopylae. The pass was chosen because it was believed to be the safest route through a part of central Greece. But at just barely 50 feet (15m) in width, the pass proved to be a formidable obstacle. A contingent of just three hundred Greek warriors from Sparta occupied the narrow pass. This small force prevented the much larger Persian army from proceeding. A fierce fight broke out that stopped the Persian advance for several days until a Greek traitor told the Persians about a goat trail leading around the pass. The next day all three hundred Spartans were killed, and the Persians continued down the coast along with their fleet toward Athens.

The Destruction of Athens

When the Persians entered Athens, they found the city vacant. Most Athenians had evacuated the city, taking refuge on Salamis Island, just off the coast a few miles. The Persian general Mardonius ordered the destruction of the city, beginning with the most sacred temples on the Acropolis, the hill that rises high above the city. But as his army made its way up the steep path, a small number of patriotic Athenians hiding on the summit viciously attacked, as Herodotus describes in his book *The Persian Wars*:

> They stoutly refused [to surrender] and among their other modes of defense, rolled down huge masses of stone upon the barbarians as they were mounting up to the gates: so that Xerxes was for a long time very greatly perplexed, and could not contrive any way to take them.

HERODOTUS: THE FATHER OF HISTORY

The great fifth-century Greek historian Herodotus is today revered as "the Father of History" because he was the first Western historian to compile a comprehensive history that attempted to be fair and accurate. The opening lines of his book *The Persian Wars* explain to the reader why he is writing his history:

> These are the researches of Herodotus of Halicarnassus [a city on the Ionian coast], which he publishes, in the hope of thereby preserving from decay the remembrance of what men have done, and of preventing the great and wonderful actions of the Greeks and the Barbarians [Persians] from losing their due meed [portion] of glory; and withal to put on record what were their grounds of feuds.

As a historian, Herodotus is both admired and criticized by modern historians. He is admired because he was the first to attempt some degree of objectivity. He explains, for example, that although he was born after the Persian wars, he interviewed Greeks who fought in order to gather first-hand information and he visited the battle sites. He further explains that when he received contradictory accounts of events from those who participated, he carefully weighed the merits of each account before selecting the most reasonable one. In this regard, Herodotus brought a semblance of impartial scientific inquiry to his work.

His work, however, is not without criticism. Herodotus is prone to exaggerate in a way that reveals his bias favoring the Greeks over the Persians. He also frequently calls the reader's attention to the weak moral character of the Persians and their indulgence in decadent lifestyles valuing riches and vice over the Greek lifestyle valuing modest living and high moral character.

Herodotus is known as "the Father of History" for his efforts to compile a relatively balanced account of ancient Western history.

THE PERSIAN ARCHERS AT THERMOPYLAE

The Persians considered archers to be the backbone of their army. Historians recording many of the great Persian battles often praised the archers and their deadly accuracy. According to Herodotus in his book *The Persian War*, Xerxes boasted, "I will conquer Greece with my archers."

One of the most remarkable battle scenes recorded by Herodotus in which archers played a major and dramatic role was at the Battle of Thermopylae. According to his story, the Persians were prevented from passing through the mountain pass at Thermopylae. Out of desperation, a general ordered his archers to dislodge the Spartans holding the pass with their arrows. According to Herodotus:

> A speech which he [the Spartan Dieneces] made before the Greeks engaged the Persians, remains on record. One of the Trachinians [from the city of Trachis] told him, "Such was the number of the barbarians, that when they shot forth their arrows the sun would be darkened by their multitude." Dieneces, not at all frightened at these words, but making light of the Median numbers, answered, "Our Trachinian friend brings us excellent tidings. If the Medes darken the sun, we shall have our fight in the shade."

Despite the volume of arrows, the heavily armored Spartans were able to shield themselves from the onslaught. Apparently the Persians' lightweight arrows were not able to penetrate their armor or shields.

The arrows of the Persian archers were no match for the well-armored Spartan phalanx at Thermopylae in 480 B.C.

At last, however, in the midst of these many difficulties, the barbarians made discovery of an access. . . . Right in front of the citadel, but behind the gates and the common ascent—where no watch was kept, and no one would have thought it possible that any foot of man could climb—a few soldiers mounted from the sanctuary of Aglaurus, Cecrops's daughter, notwithstanding the steepness of the precipice. As soon as the Athenians saw them upon the summit, some threw themselves headlong from the wall, and so perished; while others fled for refuge to the inner part of the temple. The Persians rushed to the gates and opened them, after which they massacred the suppliants. When all were slain, they plundered the temple, and fired every part of the citadel. Xerxes thus completely mastered Athens.[16]

Xerces' Crushing Defeat

The Athenians sent messengers asking for assistance to repel the Persian army and received offers from several city-states. Believing that the best strategy rested with warships, Pericles, the leader of the Athenians, ordered the evacuation of Athens and the fleet to prepare for battle near Salamis Island, within sight of Athens. In the fall of 480, both fleets drew up for battle. As they advanced toward each other, the ships at the center of the Greek advance suddenly rowed in reverse, and as the Persian ships pursued what they mistakenly thought was a retreat, the left and right flanks closed in on the Persian boats, crushing them.

Xerxes fled back to Persia but ordered his army to winter in Greece for one final land battle the next spring. When spring arrived, many Greek city-states rallied at Plataea with about one hundred thousand warriors, about the same number as the Persian force. Following a weeklong battle, the Greeks prevailed and the remnants of the Persian army retreated north and back across the Hellespont.

Xerxes earned the reputation as the first Persian emperor to fail to extend the boundaries of the empire. Although the Persians remained a viable empire east of the Mediterranean, they would never again challenge the Greek city-states. Xerxes returned to Sardis to rebuild the city. While there he gave up on extending the empire and instead turned his attention to administering the empire that remained. Despite the setback in Greece, Persia remained a powerful and vital empire, and Xerxes, in the tradition of Cyrus and Darius, set himself to the task of efficiently managing it and continuing the building of cities and palaces.

CHAPTER THREE

A GENIUS FOR ADMINISTRATION

Among Persia's rulers, Cyrus and Darius made the greatest military contributions to the expansion of the empire, yet it was as administrators that they made their greatest contributions to the spread of Persian civilization since a well-administered empire was vital for the survival of all that the kings had built. To that end, Cyrus and Darius effectively maintained peace within the empire, organized it into provinces called satrapies, introduced a money system, and facilitated communications across vast stretches of territory. According to historian Jim Hicks, author of *The Persians:*

> The administrative apparatus conducted by the early kings of Persia, particularly by Darius, was a marvel of workability. So solid, in fact, were the overall accomplishments of the Persians in operating their enormous political enterprise that their record can be read almost like a textbook on empire building, offering solutions—devised by experts—to most of the problems of imperial statecraft.[17]

Cyrus's Compassion for the Vanquished

A large part of Cyrus's success as a military leader was his ability to establish peaceful relations with those whom he defeated. Herodotus credits Cyrus with the wisdom of preferring peaceful diplomacy to war, quoting the king as having once said, "Force is always beside the point when subtlety will serve."[18] In addition, Cyrus's practice, rarely seen in rulers before his time, was to offer mercy to defeated kings and their subjects. Cyrus understood that if he treated the vanquished with kindness and generosity, and allowed subject peoples to retain most of their jobs, social rank, and customs, he could expect obedience in return, even after his occupying troops returned home. It is in this context that the scholar of Persian history J.M. Cook notes, "Cyrus was a great conqueror. . . . Cyrus, like Darius after him, set great store in winning the good will of the people in the lands they conquered."[19]

Cyrus first employed this tactic following his defeat of the Medes when he allowed their religious leaders to remain in place. He also pointed several Medes to positions of authority in the government he installed in the conquered nation. In addition to fostering good relations with the Medes and preventing them from rebelling, Cyrus earned their assistance against his next foe, the Lydians. And Cyrus's strategy paid off.

When he went to war against the Lydians, the Medes fought alongside Persian troops, helping assure his victory.

Cyrus's policy of goodwill toward the vanquished was most evident during his conquest of the city of Babylon. As soon as Cyrus entered the city, he posted guards at all sacred temples to prevent looting, saw to it that the marketplaces were kept open for business, and ensured that all traditional ceremonial

CYRUS'S CHARTER OF HUMAN RIGHTS CYLINDER

Part of the success of Cyrus the Great has been attributed to his caring for the well-being of those whom he conquered. His compassion was noted by Greek historians, but it was not until 1878 that an archaeological discovery corroborated the literary evidence. British archaeologists stumbled on a clay cylinder, 9 inches (23 cm) long and 4 inches (10cm) in diameter, inscribed with cuneiform text while excavating in Babylon. A translation of the unusual cylinder revealed a description of the treatment that the Babylonians received following their conquest by Cyrus. A translation of the clay cylinder, found on the Farsinet Web site, reads, in part,

> I am Cyrus, king of the world, great king, mighty king, king of Babylon. . . . When I, well-disposed, entered Babylon, . . . my numerous troops moved about [but] I did not allow any to terrorize the land of Sumer and Akkad. I kept in view the needs of Babylon and all its sanctuaries to promote their well-being. The citizens of Babylon . . . I lifted their unbecoming yoke. Their dilapidated dwellings I restored. I put an end to their misfortunes. . . . I gathered together all their inhabitants and restored to them their dwellings. . . . May all the gods whom I have placed within their sanctuaries address a daily prayer in my favor, that my days may long . . .

At this point the remainder of the inscription is worn away and no more can be translated.

This clay cylinder is inscribed with cuneiform text that details Cyrus's treatment of the conquered Babylonians.

This well-worn relief from a sarcophagus shows a Persian satrap on his throne holding a scepter. Satraps were often chosen from local nobility.

practices were preserved. Herodotus informs his readers that, because of Cyrus's consideration, the Babylonians hardly noticed any change in their day-to-day lives.

Darius followed the example set by Cyrus. Several times, following the defeat of foes, Darius ordered a moratorium on taxes and mandatory military service to give them an opportunity to recover from their defeat. Once he gained confidence that an opponent would submit to his rule, he allowed them to choose local officials from their own ranks. As Professor Richard Frye of Harvard University notes in his book *The Heritage of Persia*, Cyrus set a precedent in working with his defeated enemies to create a peaceful, united empire:

> In the victories of the Persians . . . what was different was the new policy of reconciliation and together with this was the prime aim of Cyrus to establish a Pax Achaemenica [Achaemenid Peace]. . . . If one were to assess the achievements of the Achaemenid Persians, surely the concept of One World, . . . the fusion of peoples and cultures in one 'Oecumen' [family] was one of their important legacies.[20]

Once the loyalty of conquered peoples was gained, their territory would be administered as a semiautonomous state known as a satrapy. This form of governing worked well because each satrapy reflected the culture of the peoples living there. Each satrapy then contributed in a way that suited it to the life of the empire as a whole.

The Satrapy: Territorial Organization

Historians both ancient and modern are almost unanimous in agreeing that dividing the Persian Empire into satrapies was an extraordinary stroke of administrative genius. According to Herodotus, the empire at its height was organized into twenty-three satrapies, working together to maintain internal stability, contribute taxes, and help with defense.

To ensure that local populations would adhere to and respect Persian rule, the Persian king prudently selected each governor, called a satrap, from among the local noble families. Lesser positions were also filled by local men. Hundreds of administrators were needed to collect and count taxes, administer local justice, direct building projects, command local garrisons of soldiers, organize communication systems, repair bridges and roads, and perform dozens of lesser jobs. In so doing, the local populations had the impression that they were being ruled by their own countrymen rather than by some indifferent foreign bureaucrat. The king kept these satraps in power as long as they were loyal, and in several cases he even allowed them to pass on their powerful positions to their heirs.

Many loyal satraps who proved capable of maintaining the peace and collecting taxes became wealthy men on a scale second only to the Persian king himself. They lived in regal palaces attended by hundreds of servants, owned vast country estates, and traveled in elaborate style protected by armed bodyguards. According to Herodotus, Tritantaechmes, the satrap of Babylon, became one of the city's wealthiest citizens because of his position:

[Tax collectors] brought him an artaba [a 9-gallon (34L) container] of silver every day. He also had, belonging to his own private stud, besides war horses, 800 stallions and 16,000 mares, twenty to each stallion. Besides which he kept so great a number of Indian hounds, that four large villages of the plain were exempted from all other charges on condition of finding them food.[21]

The Persian king depended upon local satraps, yet he never left them unsupervised. Worries about corruption and rebellion ran high. The king hired fellow Persians whom he could trust to infiltrate the offices of satraps and spy on them. Known as "the King's ear," these individuals might investigate accounts of taxes collected, the honesty of judges, the movement of troops from one garrison to another, and whether the king's directives were being faithfully executed.

This carefully organized network of informants kept the king apprised of any irregularities and allowed him to move quickly and forcibly against any threat.

Collecting Tribute

Of all that might go wrong, the collecting of the annual tribute was high on the list. As each kingdom was conquered, the Persian king sent a delegation demanding earth and water as symbols of submission. This ritual symbolized Persian dominance over the vanquished king and his obligation to provide annual payments, called tribute, to the Persians. Tribute was not the sole source of income for the Persian king, but it generated more revenue than any other form of taxation. It was because of the payment of tributes by foreigners that the Persian people enjoyed a prosperity that built their magnificent cities, provided them with slave labor, paid for their armies, and stocked their homes with exotic goods from throughout the empire and even beyond.

The amount of tribute paid and the form of payment were unique for each satrapy. The king assessed tribute based on the ability of the satrapy to pay. For example, wealthier satrapies, such as Babylon and Egypt, paid more than poorer ones such as Parthia and Bactria. Satrapies such as India, with large populations, also paid more than nations with small ones. The Persian king was careful not to overburden conquered peoples, fearing that they might revolt if pressed too hard.

Tribute was usually calculated in gold and silver, but sometimes slaves were recorded in the official lists, as were exotic commodities such as foods, spices, animals, animal hides, and lumber. Twentieth-century archaeologists excavating at the ruins of Darius I's capital, Persepolis, discovered beautifully executed low-relief sculptures on the building identified as the royal treasury depicting delegations from throughout the empire bearing pots filled with gold. Of even greater interest were thirty thousand cuneiform tablets, called the Fortification Tablets, that reveal details of tribute and how the palace was administered between the years 506 and 497 B.C. They are one of the most important sources for studying the administration of the Persian Empire.

Herodotus is another source providing insights into tribute. He records money, goods, and even humans comprising tribute. He tells his readers, for example, that the Indian

The figures on this staircase from Darius's palace in Persepolis represent conquered peoples paying tribute to the Persian emperor.

satrapy paid the highest tribute because "the Indians, who are more numerous than any other nation with which we are acquainted, paid a tribute exceeding that of every other people, to wit, three hundred and sixty talents [a standardized weight] of gold." From the Egyptian satrap came a combination of money and goods: "The tribute which came in was seven hundred [silver] talents. These seven hundred talents did not include the profits of the fisheries of Lake Moeris [located in northern Egypt west of the Nile River], nor the corn [grain] furnished to the troops at Memphis. Corn was supplied to 120,000 Persians. . . . The Cilicians gave three hundred and sixty white horses, one for each day in the year, and five hundred talents of silver." And, "from Babylonia, and the rest of Assyria, were drawn a thousand talents of silver, and five hundred boy-eunuchs [castrated boys]."[22] Other unusual tribute recorded by Herodotus includes two hundred ebony logs, five Ethiopian boys, twenty elephant tusks, one hundred boys and one hundred girls, and 6,000 pounds (2,724kg) of the aromatic herb frankincense.

The disposition of tribute was at the king's discretion. Some of the money and

THE BEHISTUN INSCRIPTION

The Behistun inscription is one of the most significant archaeological finds associated with the Persian Empire. It is a long text that is engraved on a cliff about 300 feet (91m) above a road between the modern city of Hamadan, Iran, and Baghdad, Iraq, near the town of Bisotun. In its entirety, the inscription is roughly 81 feet by 50 feet (25 by 15m).

The massive inscription consists of four panels: a low-relief sculpture 18 feet by 10 feet (5.5 by 3m) depicting a life-size Darius looking down on conquered kings rendered with nooses around their necks, and three cuneiform panels written in three different languages—Elamite, Old Persian, and Babylonian. All three languages tell the identical story about Darius's choice as king by the gods and his many military conquests.

For centuries after the fall of the Persian Empire the inscription was known to exist, but the written languages had been forgotten. In 1835 Henry Rawlinson, a young English soldier, took up the task of deciphering the then-strange languages in which the inscriptions were written. By comparing the same proper nouns in each of the three languages, he was able to solve the puzzle and decipher the three languages. The significance of the Behistun inscription lies not only in the story it tells but also in its role in leading to the deciphering of three ancient lost languages.

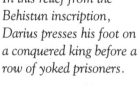

In this relief from the Behistun inscription, Darius presses his foot on a conquered king before a row of yoked prisoners.

goods he kept for his personal use, but the vast bulk was turned over to administrators who determined its distribution. Most of the tribute was spent on building or main- taining infrastructure such as buildings, roads, bridges, and boats, but some, espe- cially barges filled with wheat, goats, fruits, and vegetables, was handed out to Persian citizens who lived well because, as Herodotus points out, they paid neither tribute nor taxes: "Persia alone has not been reckoned among the tributaries—for this reason, because the country of the Persians is altogether exempt from tax."[23]

A Network of Roads

One of the highest priorities when it came to expenditures for tribute money was roads. With an empire as vast as Persia's, the need to move messages, goods, and troops quickly and efficiently was of paramount importance. First Cyrus and then Darius and Xerxes committed huge sums of money to create a network of roads that fanned out from each major city and connected them to one another and to the edges of the empire. Kings, builders, generals, merchants, farmers, bankers, and a variety of other tradespeople depended on roads for the transport of goods that supported their livelihoods.

The initial purpose for expending a large percentage of their king's treasury on roads was to increase the empire's military effectiveness by shortening the times required to move troops and supplies to a particular location. Inevitably, the same roads provided the same advantage for merchants and others who needed to move men and materials from place to place.

Every Persian king ordered local peoples under the direction of their engineers to expand and improve existing caravan routes, which were known to be rough and uneven. The engineers, using surveying tools, laid out direct routes to straighten zigzagging roads. Other times they would plot routes around mountains so that travelers would not have to force pack animals to climb

them. Under the engineers' supervision, slaves laid paving stones in marshy areas to prevent wagon and chariot wheels from disappearing into the mud. Numerous ancient accounts make it clear, however, that although they were the world's best, these roads mostly were only packed dirt and, during the winter months, it was common for wagon wheels to become stuck deep in the mud. Even vehicles belonging to the nobility were not immune, as Xenophon makes clear:

> Once in particular, when they came upon a narrow, muddy place which was hard for the wagons to get through, Cyrus halted with his train of nobles and dignitaries and ordered . . . some of the barbarian troops to pull the wagons out. But it seemed to him that they took their time with the work; accordingly, as if in anger, he directed the Persian nobles who accompanied him to take a hand in hurrying on the wagons.[24]

The most famous of all roads was the Royal Road that ran the 1,700 miles (2,735km) from Susa to Sardis. The Royal Road was the most-used road in the empire and was maintained by a small army of engineers and laborers. Herodotus, who saw the road, commented on its four ferryboat crossings at rivers, guarded checkpoints, relay stations for the royal messenger service's horses, and more than one hundred inns to feed and house weary voyagers at night. To help travelers survive crossings of long stretches of searing hot desert, large 6-foot-tall (2m) ceramic jugs were sunk in holes and filled with water. Foot travelers averaging 20 miles (32km) a day could cover the length of the Royal Road in about three months.

The Royal Messenger Service

Speedy communications between the king and his generals, satraps, and other administrative assistants were crucial for the smooth and efficient running of the empire. Even with the excellent system of roads, royal dispatches between the king and his satraps needed to move faster than someone on foot could carry them. Accordingly, a special agency called the Royal Messenger Service was instituted. The king decreed that relay stations be placed at intervals equivalent to the distance a horse can run at a moderate speed without collapsing from fatigue, about 14 miles (23km). When a message was dispatched, the relay system operated night and day, making it possible for news to travel 240 miles (386km) per day. Herodotus confirms this, reporting that a royal message traveling from Susa to Sardis was delivered in seven days. This

THE DARIUS CANAL

One of the grander administrative projects of Darius focused on opening the empire to trade with foreign lands. To facilitate trade between Persia, Egypt, and the Mediterranean, Darius dug a canal connecting the Red Sea with the Mediterranean for large freighters. To accomplish this feat, his engineers recommended the canal link the northern tip of the Red Sea with the Nile River to the west. Then from the Nile, all ships could sail north to ports on the eastern Mediterranean.

According to Herodotus, who saw the canal, it was 86 miles (138km) long, wide enough for two war galleys to pass each other under oar (about 150 feet [46m]), and ships took four days to move from one end to the other.

No evidence of the canal exists, but Herodotus claimed that Darius had ordered a special stone stele erected in commemoration of the canal. Historians were skeptical about the canal, as well as the stele, until 1866, when workers unearthed a red granite stele that stood nearly 10 feet (3m) tall and 7 feet (2m) wide carved in Old Persian, Babylonian, Elamite, and Egyptian. The inscription, which is cited in A.T. Olmstead's book *History of the Persian Empire*, reads, "I commanded this canal to be dug from the river, Nile by name, which flows in Egypt, to the sea which goes from Persia. Afterward this canal was dug as I commanded, ships passed from Egypt through this canal to Persia as was my will."

time is remarkable when compared to the three months that it took caravans of wagons carrying goods to travel that same route. Herodotus elaborates on the Persian communication system:

> Nothing mortal travels so fast as these Persian messengers. The entire plan is a Persian invention; and this is the method of it. Along the whole line of road there are men stationed with horses. . . . The first rider delivers his dispatch to the second and the second passes it to the third; and so it is borne from hand to hand along the whole line.[25]

The royal messenger service was more than swift; it was also renowned for its reliability. A lost or delayed message could cost a general a crucial victory or a condemned man being pardoned by the king his life. Riders, therefore, were handpicked for their bravery, perseverance, and willingness to sacrifice their lives to deliver a royal message, as Herodotus notes: "These men will not be hindered from accomplishing at their best speed the distance which they have to go, either by snow, or rain, or heat, or by the darkness of night."[26]

Sometimes the need for a quick response to a simple message required speeds even faster than horses. To serve in such circumstances, signal towers were constructed on high vantage points such as mountain peaks where royal messengers used fires to send messages. Historians speculate that messages were communicated using a type of code similar to the modern Morse code. The signalmen would light a large bonfire and then screen the fire—on and off—from the view of lookouts manning the next hilltop outpost. Once the message was received, it was passed on in similar fashion to the next tower until it reached its destination.

By employing riders and signal fires, the Persian king was able to remain abreast of any breaking news of trouble within the immense empire. Within hours of a problem occurring, Persian officials could head it off by dispatching troops or other assistance before the problem could spin out of control.

Implementing a Money System

Another necessity for the smooth administration of the empire was a standard currency. Trading goods and services, known as bartering, worked fine for small villages, but an empire needed a more reliable money system. According to Herodotus, who was fascinated with the workings of the Persian Empire, Darius was the first Persian king to implement a money system based on coins. This system, based on the example set by the Lydian king Croesus, was a significant improvement over the more chaotic, simpler, and more primitive system of barter because coins had a set value recognized by everyone, whereas goods and services did not.

The largest standard unit of money was the talent, and its use spread throughout the ancient world and lasted for hundreds of years. The Persian talent weighed 66 pounds (30kg) and could be of either silver or gold. Archaeologists have uncovered several of them cast in the shape of a disk. Historians struggled to understand the purchasing power of a talent until discovering one reference to a silver talent being sufficient to pay a two-hundred-man crew of rowers for one

This gold coin bears a likeness of King Darius in battle. Darius was the first Persian ruler to introduce a standard currency.

month and a gold talent to purchase an entire warship. Purchases of goods and services such as these were transactions carried out by governments, but something else was needed for the average citizen. To address the needs of shoppers and merchants, small coins were struck. This work was performed by the king's mint exclusively to ensure standard weight and purity. The first standard coin, the *daric*, was named either for Darius or after the Persian word for gold, *dari*. Thousands of these coins have been excavated and analyzed by archaeologists called numismatists, who specialize in studying coins. The *daric* is .75 inches (1.9cm) in diameter, weighs 33 ounces (935g), and contains 98 percent gold and 2 percent silver and nickel to harden it. One inscription from the time of Darius records the sale of one healthy ox for one gold daric. Less valuable coins, such as the silver *daric*, were also minted, as were gold and silver *sigoli;* twenty *sigoli* equaled one *daric*.

Coins circulating throughout the empire were useful not just for what they could purchase but for projecting the king's image.

One of the earliest coins of interest to numismatists depicts Darius in profile wearing a crown and a long beard and kneeling while holding a spear and bow. Others depict the king on one side of the coin sitting on his horse and an impressive animal such as a lion or a bear standing upright on the other side.

Sophisticated administration was the backbone of the empire, along with the military. The efficient administration not only held the empire together, but it also made life at the court of the king pleasurable and entertaining for his entourage of wealthy families.

CHAPTER FOUR

LIFE AT THE COURT OF THE GREAT KINGS

The court of the king, which consisted of the king's family, trusted nobles, and servants, was a source of fascination for foreign observers such as Herodotus. Thanks to accounts such as his, coupled with recent archaeological discoveries, students of Persian history have available a rich trove of information regarding the secluded world of the king's court.

The King's Palaces

When a king was not actually at war, he took pleasure in boasting of his conquests. Often, the boasting came in the form of constructing royal palaces that reflected in size and elaborate decorations the king's importance. The largest and best known are those built at the five royal cities that served at various times as the capital of the Persian Empire: Susa, Babylon, Pasargadae, Ecbatana, and Persepolis.

At each of these cities the palace was built in a grandiose architectural style termed *monumental* by modern archaeologists. This term most of all describes their massive size yet additionally suggests the wealth of expensive materials used in construction and the importance of its occupants. In any case, the royal residence had to be monumental to accommodate the king and his courtly entourage which, along with all of his attendants and bodyguards, is estimated to have been as many as twelve thousand.

Of the five palaces, the one at Persepolis, located 25 miles (40km) northeast of the modern city of Shīrāz in modern Iran, has surrendered the most spectacular finds to archaeologists. Based on what has been uncovered, archaeologists have been able to determine the size of the palace, the number and function of major structures, the materials used in its construction, and the sculptures depicting life at the court of the king. Begun by Darius around 520 B.C., Persepolis was not completed until a century later. The first remarkable feature of Persepolis revealed by excavators was a massive 1.5-million-square-foot (139,000 sq. m) stone and dirt foundation set 46 feet (14m) above the desert floor to create a level platform for the nine major buildings that comprised the palace complex. So massive was this foundation that it took five hundred laborers using shovels and trucks three years to unearth it. Rising an additional 50 feet (15m) above the perimeter of the foundation was a stone fortification wall with guard towers built from blocks of stone 24 by 7 by 9 feet (7 by 2 by 3 m). Access to the palace complex was discovered to be a monumental staircase from the desert floor to the entry gate named the Gate of All Lands. This entry gate, still largely intact, is flanked by twin 18-foot-tall (5.5m) carved limestone bulls (one now headless) and a complex of 60-foot (18m) tall columns that once supported a roof.

Of the nine buildings on the terrace, the one that exemplifies monumental architecture more than any other is the Apadana, a term meaning "The Great Reception Hall" in Elamite, the official spoken language of the Persians. This massive yet elegant square structure, with an interior space of 180,000 square feet (16,723 sq. m), was the largest and most magnificent of all the palace buildings at Persepolis. Archaeologists have been able to stabilize thirteen of its seventy-two carved limestone columns that originally stood on its enormous platform supporting a wooden-beam

This aerial view of the ruins of Darius's palace at Persepolis gives some idea of its massive size. It was one of the many palaces built by Persian rulers.

This artist's rendering of Persepolis shows how it looked in its heyday.

roof covered with ceramic tiles. The two staircases accessing the building have been restored to reveal simple yet gracefully executed low-relief sculptures depicting scenes from a new year's festival. The other major structures at Persepolis include two king's residences (one built by Darius and the other by Xerxes), the apartments of the king's concubines, the royal treasury, the royal council hall, the king's throne hall, and the tomb of Artaxerxes.

The Royal Processional

As elaborate as a palace complex might be, it was only occupied part of each year. During the course of a year the king and his entire court might move several times. Everywhere the king went, he required an elaborate escort of soldiers, royal attendants, his horses, and his chariot and driver. Part of the mystique that the king projected when he rode in processionals was the notion that he could only be viewed by his subjects from afar. With this in mind, the king never allowed commoners to approach him. To keep curious commoners at a distance, yet impress them with his regal magnificence, the king only traveled in majestic royal processionals.

Herodotus's descriptions of several elaborate processionals indicate that they were meant both to protect the king and to underscore his preeminence. Herodotus describes a processional conducted for King Xerxes:

In front of the king went first 1,000 horsemen, picked men of the Persian nation—then spearmen, 1,000, like-wise chosen troops, with their spear-heads pointing towards the ground—next ten of the sacred horses called Nisaean. Next to this came Xerxes himself riding in a chariot drawn by Nisaean horses, with his charioteer Patiramphes. Immediately behind the king there followed a body of 1,000 spearmen, then 1,000 Persian horsemen, then 10,000 serving on foot. Of these, 1,000 carried spears with golden pomegranates at

their lower end instead of spikes, 9,000 with silver pomegranates, and 1,000 Persians with golden apples.[27]

Historical inscriptions describe, and low-relief sculptures depict, the king riding in a specially designed chariot. Processional chariots were readily distinguishable from war chariots by their greater size. They had dual axles for their four wheels and a large, heavy chassis to hold the king and his royal charioteer, who drove the eight horses. The extremes to which the king went to demonstrate his privileged position was highlighted by one writer, who notes "Whenever the king descended from his chariot, he never leaped down, although the distance to the ground was short, nor did he lean on anyone's arm; rather, a golden stool was set in place for him, and he descended stepping on this; and the king's stool-bearer attended him for this purpose."[28]

Herodotus sometimes touches on other odd aspects of processionals such as this one describing Xerxes as he was about to cross a bridge: "All that day the preparations for the passage continued; and on the morning they burnt all kinds of spices upon the bridge, and strewed the way with myrtle boughs."[29]

PALACE LOW-RELIEF SCULPTURES

Art historians call the form of sculptures excavated from the great royal cities of the Persian Empire low-relief sculptures. This means that the object sculpted projects only slightly from the stone, often little more than 2 to 4 inches (5 to 10cm). Unlike Greek freestanding sculptures, which are truly three dimensional and allow the viewer to circle statues to see them revealed in 360 degrees, low-relief sculptures are relatively flat and reveal only slightly more than 180 degrees of surface.

The finest examples of Persian low-relief sculptures are found in all of the royal cities and their palaces. Typically, the depictions were carved into enormous slabs of stone, often granite or basalt, many feet long and tall. Without the ability to sculpt in 360 degrees, the faces of people and animals are always in profile.

The low-relief sculptures typically depict elaborate processions of one sort or another. At Persepolis, for example, a procession of tribute bearers adorns the great double staircase approaching the audience hall of Xerxes. In this rendering, dozens of young bearded men carry over their shoulders containers

filled with valuables for the king. The men's beards are rendered as curls with small holes drilled to give the impression of thickness. At Susa, another famous processional called the Processional of Archers is sculpted in enameled brick. Each archer is identical, holding a spear in the left hand and a bow and quiver filled with arrows over the shoulder.

Pictured here is a relief known as the Processional of the Archers found in Darius's palace at Susa.

The carving on this silver plaque depicts a Persian hunting scene. Persian royalty hunted in special parks that were well stocked with game animals.

Another activity demonstrating the lavish lifestyle of the king was a favorite royal sport, hunting. As was the case with the processionals, royal hunts were lavish affairs reserved for the king and his entourage.

The Royal Hunt

The royal hunts were described by several Greek historians who claimed to have witnessed them. Xenophon, for example, notes in the *Anabasis*, "In Celaenae, . . . Cyrus had a palace and a large park full of wild animals, which he used to hunt on horseback

whenever he wished to give himself and his horses exercise."[30] Hunts took place in royal parks, called *paradeisos* by the Greeks who witnessed them. There, guards were stationed to prevent commoners from entering. Each hunt required meticulous attention to duties carried out by men specifically tasked to ensure an exciting hunt. Wild animals such as bears, deer, lions, and gazelles were caged and well fed before the hunt. The selected animals were then released from their cages and allowed a head start before the king's hunting dogs

This relief depicts servants serving food at a funeral banquet. Persian royalty hosted lavish banquets to celebrate a number of occasions.

were released. Finally the king and his entourage set out on horseback.

The thrill of the hunt was the chase across the open fields, splashing across streams, and darting through thick brush under potentially dangerous low-lying tree branches. Xenophon claims as many as five hundred horsemen took part in a hunt in addition to the king's bodyguards, who were obliged to follow him to discourage would-be assassins. Once the quarry was located and run down, dogs moved in for the kill, as did riders armed with bows and arrows and spears.

Royal Banquets

Each hunt ended with a banquet attended by the hunters and their families. Hunting banquets were but one of the many types of banquets held at the court; the nobles dressed in their finest clothes and sat in anticipation of exotic foods, service, and entertainment. With the possible exception of the palaces of the kings, royal banquets fascinated ancient writers more than any other extravagance associated with Persian royalty. Banquets had long been an ancient tradition as religious celebrations at which the noble families gathered for prayer, animal sacrifice, and austere dining. But as the power of the king increased, banquets became yet one more ostentatious demonstration of his unchallenged wealth and authority. Banquets were held at palaces to celebrate annual Persian religious events, but a king might also call for one for no particular reason—even while in the midst of a military campaign and far from home.

Modern historians attempting to reconstruct accurately the foods offered at the king's banquet table are in agreement that meats, breads, wines, and fruits were in plentiful supply. The offering of meats always included fowl (geese, peacock, duck, pigeon) and either lamb or goat, but on occasion gazelle and giraffe were included, and, on rare occasions, fish. A variety of breads were served depending upon the availability of grains, but wheat and barley were standards. As for wines, Xenophon informs his readers that "the Persian king has vintners scouring every land to find some drink that will tickle his palate."[31] Fruits were popular because they were sweet, moist, and plentiful. A traditional fruit platter included figs, dates, pomegranates, apples, and raisins. Occasionally honey was drizzled over the fruit to add sweetness. Other than this use of honey over fruit, however, how these foods were prepared is entirely lost to historians. No recipes have survived, although a large variety of spices are reported in kitchen inventories inscribed on clay tablets.

Banquet table settings rivaled the foods for splendor. One description provided by Herodotus describes the surprise of the Greek Pausanius, who saw a Persian banquet table inside a tent:

Xerxes, when he fled away out of Greece, left his war-tent with Mardonius: when Pausanias, therefore, saw the tent with its adornments of gold and silver, and its hangings of divers colors, he gave commandment to the bakers and the cooks to make him ready a banquet in such fashion as was their wont for Mardonius. Then they made ready as they were bidden; and Pausanius, beholding the couches of gold and silver daintily decked out with their rich covertures, and the tables of gold and silver laid, and the feast itself prepared with all magnificence, was astonished at the good things which were set before him.[32]

Banquets were social events, and where a guest sat at the table relative to the king was a mark of that individual's importance. The king could honor or dishonor a man simply by moving him closer to or farther from the royal seat.

As lavish as the table setting was, the only eating utensil was a knife, and each guest brought his or her own. Meats were picked by hand from serving platters, cut into pieces, placed on bread, and consumed. Some diners who chose not to use knives simply used their hands and teeth to tear large pieces of meat into smaller ones. Shirtsleeves served as napkins, and the points of knives served as toothpicks. The floor was the receptacle for bones and other uneaten scraps.

The archaeological record corroborates some of the descriptions provided by writers at the time. Low-relief sculptures excavated at Susa, Persepolis, and Pasargadae depict banquets that include a procession of lambs and goats pulled by ropes up ramps toward the banquet tables just before their slaughter. The animals are followed by hundreds of servants mounting a stairway, bearing goatskins presumably filled with wine and water. These servants are followed by bare-chested young men holding serving dishes filled with breads and fruits.

The Women of the Palace

Life at the court, including banquets, was largely oriented toward the king and his male advisers, although women are mentioned by historians. Whereas only a handful of influential women played significant roles at the court, thousands of other women played insignificant yet necessary roles as well. Large numbers of women, in addition to those who were family members, shared the palace with the king and his entourage. Historical sources indicate four prominent categories of women: the king's wife or wives, whose function was to bear the king an official heir; concubines, who provided the king with sexual pleasure; courtesans, who provided cultural entertainment; and the domestics, palace servants who cleaned and attended to the everyday needs of the king and his court.

Among the women, standing at the apex of the palace's social pyramid was the queen or queens. Polygamy was a common practice for Persian kings who married noble women. The purpose of a royal marriage was to produce an heir to the throne or cement a strategic alliance with another king—or both. Only children born to one of the queens stood to inherit their father's throne and vast wealth.

Just below the queens in the royal pecking order were the king's concubines. Differ-

ent kings had different numbers of concubines, and one was reputed to have had 360, one for every day of the Persian year. Concubines were either slaves purchased at auction or young women seized as spoils of war following a military victory. Herodotus claims that following the defeat of some Ionian towns, "the most beautiful of the girls they [the Persians] tore from their homes and sent as presents to the king."[33] According to the Greek writer Plutarch, "When the Persian kings take their dinner, the lawful wives sit beside them and eat with them. But when the kings wish to be merry and get drunk, they send their wives away, and send for their music—girls and concubines."[34]

The concubines were treated almost as well as the royal women. At the palace, concubines enjoyed luxurious accommodations. Also when the kings went on long hunts or distant travel, they always took several carriage loads of concubines with them. Any children a king fathered with a concubine might be guaranteed a leisurely life at the court, but nothing more. It was commonplace for kings to father many more illegitimate children than legitimate ones; one king had 3 legitimate children and 111 illegitimate ones.

Below the concubines in status were the courtesans. These women, who were also slaves, were usually trained to play musical instruments, sing, and dance. Their role was to provide polite entertainment that could be enjoyed during banquets and other celebrations.

At the bottom of the female hierarchy were the domestics, who provided the maid services for the palace. Most domestics were women taken as prisoners of war. They were

THE TEN THOUSAND IMMORTALS

Persian kings felt the need for one contingent of superior fighting men whose loyalty and fighting skills were above all others. Their charter, in addition to fighting on the battlefield, was to serve as the contingent that guarded the king's palaces and acted as his personal bodyguard.

Cyrus created an elite core of fighters made up exclusively of loyal Persians called the Ten Thousand Immortals. As their name suggests, their number was never allowed to fall below ten thousand, as Herodotus explains in his history *The Persian Wars:* "They were called 'the Immortals,' for the following reason. If one of their body failed either by the stroke of death or of disease, forthwith his place was filled up by another man, so that their number was at no time either greater or less than 10,000."

The gallantry and fierceness of the Ten Thousand Immortals were displayed in battles against many nations, and their reputation spread throughout the empire. The Persians won some battles simply by displaying the Ten Thousand Immortals on the battlefield in full view of the enemy, which was sometimes willing to surrender rather than face certain defeat.

The ferocity of the Ten Thousand was well rewarded. Herodotus describes their unique status, noting "They were followed by litters, wherein rode their

concubines, and by a numerous train of attendants handsomely dressed. Camels and sumpter-beasts [pack animals] carried their provision, apart from that of the other soldiers."

These two members of the elite Ten Thousand Immortals were immortalized in a relief found at the palace at Persepolis.

THE PALACE PHYSICIAN

Physicians played an unusual role at the king's palace. Their loyalty was beyond reproach because they were in the unique position of being able to kill the king either with poison or by surgery. Ancient historians have mentioned several physicians who attended to medical problems encountered by kings.

The two most common problems requiring medical attention were injuries related to falls from horses and from war. During a hunt, Darius fell from his horse and twisted his ankle. His Egyptian physician was unable to reduce the swelling, so Darius acquired the assistance of a Greek physician named Democedes. Democedes restored the king's use of his foot, and Darius rewarded him with a house and a place at the king's table.

If the king or any of his immediate family were wounded on the battlefield, they were attended by the physician who traveled with the king. One account of a noble being attended on the battlefield, recorded by Herodotus, indicates that a spear wound was dressed with myrrh (an effective antimicrobial herb) and wrapped in linen bandages.

In addition to attending to the king, the royal physician attended the king's wives during birth. Doctors also performed amputations with a sharp knife to cut the skin, a sword to break the bone, and a hot iron to cauterize the stump.

forced to work cooking, cleaning, washing, and caring for the personal needs of women of higher rank or anyone else who made demands on them. On a few occasions, references are made to domestics providing daily care for royal children. Ancient texts tell of several thousand domestics working in each of the king's five palaces. Domestics were assigned a single responsibility in one part of the palace, but because of their numbers, there was no room in the palace itself for them to live. Instead, they lived in nearby complexes of simple houses.

Regardless of the status of any woman in the palace, all—even the queen—were considered to be possessions of the king. They played no role in decisions made about them or their future. As an example, royal daughters were often used to cement relationships between two powerful royal families through their marriage to young princes. Being a princess did not guarantee royal marriage, though. According to the historian J.M. Cook, the king's daughters "could even be bestowed on high Persian nobles as a reward for good service."[35]

Some accounts, especially in the form of cuneiform tablets and coins excavated at Persepolis, describe women of the palace engaged in challenging activities despite their second-class status. Coins have recently been unearthed depicting women on horseback taking part in the hunt, receiving guests at royal meetings, and even carrying weapons. The tablets also refer to women being educated in mathematics, astronomy, and literature. These recent archaeological revelations suggest to modern scholars that some women within the palace accomplished more than merely caring for the needs of the men.

Eunuchs

Women were not alone in providing for the daily needs of the king and the nobility. There were some jobs that required physical strength, fighting skills, and unwavering loyalty. For these jobs, a special corps of men, eunuchs, was chosen. Eunuchs were castrated men who, because they could not father children, filled the king's need for strong men capable of fighting off attackers yet who would not arouse suspicions regarding the legitimacy of the children the queen bore. The role of eunuchs later expanded to include guarding the king's concubines and eventually the king's entire family.

All eunuchs were slaves either taken as spoils of war or purchased at slave markets. Ancient sources report that the market for eunuchs was brisk and that the most physically attractive were taken as young boys, castrated, and shipped to markets throughout the empire. One ancient Greek historian reports that eunuchs were even wagered as stakes in a game of dice played between King Artaxerxes and his mother, Queen Parysatis: "She pressed him to begin a new game for a eunuch; to which he consented . . . and that the loser would yield up any the winner should make choice of."[36]

A second attribute that eunuchs offered

to a king was that their inability to have children precluded developing obligations or emotional ties to their own families. Instead, eunuchs who were treated well would, in theory, establish emotional ties and a sense of obligation to the king. This point was emphasized by Xenophon, who reported this observation about Cyrus:

> Those, therefore, who had children or congenial wives or sweethearts, such he believed, were by nature constrained to love them best. But as he observed that eunuchs were not susceptible to any such affections, he thought that they would esteem most highly those who were in the best position to make them rich and to stand by them, if ever they were wronged, and to place them in offices of honor; and no one, he thought, could surpass him in bestowing favors of that kind.[37]

Over time, eunuchs assumed an increasingly important role in court life. They earned a reputation for trustworthiness and loyalty that went beyond the bedroom. Kings readily relied on them as advisers, teachers for the royal children, accountants, and even personal representatives who traveled through the empire and reported back to the king. Some kings even counted a few eunuchs among their closest and most loyal friends and confidants.

As their trust was earned, a few eunuchs gained tremendous wealth and influence. One such eunuch, Bagoas, gained so much notoriety that Artaxerxes III made him a satrap. According to one historian of the time, "The king no longer decided anything without his advice."[38] As Bagoas's power grew, however, he became as powerful as the king. Finally, he assassinated Artaxerxes along with the king's brother and installed a friend of his on the throne. But soon unhappy with the new king, Bagoas killed him and installed yet another, who, as soon as he was crowned, immediately turned on Bagoas and poisoned him.

Life at the courts of the great kings was an unparalleled experience in extravagant living for the royal family and the nobility. These individuals were part of a minuscule percentage of the empire's immense population. For the rest, life was harsh and short. Nonetheless, millions of Persians and other nationalities pressed on with their lives trying to find some simple pleasures in their villages and with their families.

CHAPTER FIVE

EVERYDAY LIFE
IN THE
PERSIAN EMPIRE

Hard work was the ruling fact of life for the vast majority of Persians. They tilled the fields, fought the battles, and fabricated handcrafted goods for the marketplace. Few ever saw the interior of a palace. Despite lives of toil, most managed to find some simple pleasures living in ancient Persia, and most participated in many of the available cultural activities.

Going to Market

Peasants living in rural towns and villages from time to time needed to acquire things that they could not make for themselves or find locally. In thousands of larger towns throughout the empire, open-air markets were held once or twice a month so peasants could buy whatever they needed. These marketplaces, often little more than clusters of temporary tents set up on poles in the center of town, in addition to providing opportunities to conduct necessary business, provided the only chance for socializing that many residents of remote villages knew.

Exactly how much Persians relied on marketplaces is unclear. Herodotus states in his history that the Persians were unfamiliar with markets and did not use them. Archaeological evidence, however, indicates otherwise. A stele—a stone slab with an in-

scription or sculpture used as a monument—excavated in 1981 and dated to about 500 B.C. depicts a marketplace showing a variety of goods spread before shoppers who eye the dazzling cornucopia. Some are pointing, others are gesturing as if negotiating a price. Equally significant are large low-relief sculptures found and restored in Persepolis that depict caravans of camels weighted down with packs arriving at the main marketplace where shoppers appear to anxiously await their contents.

Moreover, Xenophon provides a glimpse into one Persian marketplace in a town preparing for war. He only mentions military paraphernalia available for sale. Nonetheless, Xenophon describes a colorful setting: "The market-place literally teemed with horses, arms, and accoutrements of all sorts for sale. The bronze-worker, the carpenter, the blacksmith, the leather-cutter, the painter, and embosser, were all busily engaged in fabricating the implements of war."[39]

Elsewhere in his writings, Xenophon records that many transactions involved unusual items and that many were acquired through trade, not purchased with money. He records a family that made millstones—large, heavy, circular stones used to grind

This fragment of a plaque shows a Persian woman spinning thread in the marketplace. The market served as the cultural center for the commoners.

grains into flour—bringing several to the marketplace and trading them for food. On another occasion Xenophon witnessed potters accepting salted fish in exchange for ceramic jars filled with olive oil. This kind of barter was more the norm in rural districts than in cities, where coinage was common.

One of the most unusual commodities to be found in many marketplaces was human beings. The slave trade was brisk during the Persian Empire, and those wealthy enough to afford a slave or two went to the market to buy them. In a special area of the market designated for slave trading, buyers could find men for hard labor on farms, women as house attendants, young girls as concubines, and eunuchs to serve as guards.

The marketplace was also a place of high adventure that provided a carnival atmosphere for women and their children. This was the place were families met for a few hours to trade stories and gossip, where children played with their cousins and grandparents and learned family traditions going back generations, and where teenagers became aware of who might soon be available for marriage. A day at the marketplace might be the only break in the routine of farmers and small craftsmen and their families.

Justice

The marketplace was an enjoyable environment for people, yet administrators reporting to the satrap kept an eye on all activities. In the event that buyers were cheated by merchants, goods were stolen, or disputes erupted into violence, there were officials on site to administer justice. Meting out justice was regarded as a critical ele-

ment in the administration of the empire. To maintain order among the populace, Persian kings established courts to resolve legal disputes.

Highest on the list of judges empowered to dispense justice were the kings themselves and their satraps. Whether sitting at their courts or moving about their realm, these high-ranking men accepted petitions from commoners asking for a ruling in a dispute. They would then read the petition and render a verdict. Xenophon tells one fascinating story about Cyrus the Great dispensing justice from his processional chariot:

Sitting on his throne, King Darius presides over a legal case. Persian kings established a court system to resolve legal disputes, with the king himself as the ultimate authority.

And as he proceeded, a great throng of people followed outside the lines with petitions to present to Cyrus, one about one matter, another about another. So he sent to them some of his mace-bearers, who followed, three on either side of his chariot, for the express purpose of carrying messages for him; and he bade them say that if any one wanted anything of him, he should make his wish known to some one of his cavalry officers and they, he said, would inform him, and he would answer.[40]

Such instances of the king himself sitting in judgment were relatively rare. Persian justice was more often dispensed in a system of courts in which a judge presided. Judges were appointed for life unless they committed some offense. Cases these courts dealt with included disputes over inheritance, property, theft, and murder. Judges also served as juries. They would hear both sides of a dispute, listen to witnesses if there were any, and render a verdict on the spot. Their decisions were final; appeals were not allowed.

If a judge found someone guilty of a crime, he would pronounce a sentence as well. Penalties might involve nothing more than paying a fine, but many were far more severe. Persia had no jails. Punishments instead consisted of execution or torture. According to ancient observers, the forms of execution most widely used were decapitation and crucifixion. Both were intended to deter others from committing similar crimes. They were carried out in public, and in the case of decapitation, the head would be hung on the town wall or some other highly visible location to be seen by all

passersby. Crucifixion would also be carried out in public. The condemned were hung from tall poles, where they suffered a slow and painful death in full view of citizens making their way along city streets. One Greek visitor who saw such a crucifixion commented, "They were intended to catch the eye of the beholder."[41]

Punishment often involved the removal of some body part. Histories from the time contain numerous accounts of ears, noses, fingers, and hands sliced from a criminal's body. Gouging of eyes was also commonplace. Darius is cited in a cuneiform tablet as saying about one rebel he tortured, "I cut off his nose, ears, and tongue and plucked out an eye; he was chained under guard at the gate of my palace and everybody could see him there."[42] Of the many forms of torture, one of the more bizarre reported by the Greek historian Isocrates was that of an Egyptian who rebelled against Cambyses and was "forced to drink bull's blood; and died on the spot."[43]

Education

For ancient Persians, the justice system was just one aspect of a well-ordered society. From Cyrus to Xerxes, kings also believed that education was another key element in making their sprawling empire work. For that reason, kings sought to make education available to as many of the empire's citizens as possible.

Herodotus, Xenophon, and Strabo all make the case that education was important and available to all Persians. However, Xenophon also adds this important bit of information: "Every Persian is entitled to send his children to the public schools of righteousness and justice. As a fact, all who can af-

PERSIAN HOUSES

The climate of Persia determined the building materials and style of homes for the common people. Building materials available within Persia included brick made from straw and mud; stone; and timber for interior roof beams.

The design of simple homes, which is known from literary descriptions and from occasional etchings on stone, was a one- or two-story rectangular structure divided into two or more separate living quarters. Access to the top floor was by way of an exterior ladder. Such homes were intended to serve one or more families in separate living areas.

Walls were constructed from unbaked mud bricks mixed with straw. They were erected on a foundation of either fired bricks or stone for added strength. Archaeologists have evidence that roofs consisted of whole or split timber beams covered with reed matting, a layer of lime, and then a thick layer of mud. If families had extra money, they might plaster both the interior and exterior walls. Windows, the only source of daylight, were merely holes in the walls with wooden shutters to close during cold nights.

The interior was warmed by a single fireplace that was also used to cook meals. The floor, whether earthen, stone, or brick, might be covered with reed mats, woven carpets, or animal skins. In the homes of the very poor, the floors were compacted dirt that were simply swept clean.

---

ford to bring up their children without working do send them there: those who cannot must forgo the privilege."[44] In other words, education was available only to the relatively well to do, certainly not to the children of peasants. Additional discussions of education scattered throughout Xenophon's book also make it clear that this privilege was available to boys but not girls.

Both Herodotus and Xenophon discuss several stages of a boy's education. Herodotus makes this simple observation: "Their sons are carefully instructed from their fifth to their twentieth year, in three things alone—to ride, to draw the bow, and to speak the truth. Until their fifth year they are not allowed to come into the sight of their father, but pass their lives with the women."[45] Fortunately for modern scholars, Strabo provides a fuller description of a Persian education. He presents a picture of boys well disciplined and trained in the arts of war, hunting, and agriculture:

> The youths are called to rise before day-break, at the sound of brazen

GOLD RHYTONS

Some of the most remarkable and highly prized artifacts recovered by archaeologists are solid gold drinking cups called rhytons. These decorative cups provide a glimpse into how the rich lived as well as the high quality of Persian craftsmanship.

Unique to the rhyton was its shape. Each rhyton had two distinct parts: a sculpted end featuring either an animal head and forequarters, such as a lion or a mythical animal like a griffin, and a cup end. The cup, into which some drink was poured, was attached at a right angle to the animal's back. The rendering of the animal portion of the rhyton is what makes it the most valued gold artifact from the Achaemenid period. Whether a lion or a griffin, details of the face, teeth, snarling open mouth, and front claws are superbly crafted. Many have a hole drilled into the front legs that connects to the cup. The hole was covered with the drinker's fingers to prevent the liquid from spilling out, but when he or she wanted to take a drink, the finger was removed and the foreleg portion brought to the lips.

Archaeologists specializing in gold artifacts have concluded that the gold rhytons were created by hammering, engraving, soldering, and riveting together its many parts. The upright cup was attached to the animal by rivets.

This solid gold drinking cup known as a rhyton features a superbly cast ram at one end.

instruments, and assemble in one spot, as if for arming themselves or for the chase. . . . At command [they] run an appointed distance of thirty or forty stadia [7.5 or 10 miles; 12 or 16km]. . . . They are taught to endure heat, cold, and rains; to cross torrents, and keep their armor and clothes dry; to pasture animals, to watch all night in the open air, and to eat wild fruits. . . . Their mode of hunting is by throwing spears from horseback, or with the bow or the sling. In the evening they are employed in planting trees, cutting roots, fabricating armor, and making lines and nets.[46]

Work

Education may have been for the more affluent members of society, but work was expected of everyone. Not many choices were available, and most children had little choice other than to follow in the footsteps of their parents.

Ancient chroniclers speak of several categories of work performed by the common people, but they make it clear that agriculture was the backbone of the empire's economy. The bulk of the population lived in the country and earned their livelihood cultivating the soil. Free farmers rarely owned more land than they could till, generally between 4 and 10 acres (1.6 and 4 ha). Parcels were referred to as "bow land" because how much land a farmer could own was often determined by how far a man could shoot an arrow with his bow.

Cuneiform tax records uncovered during excavations of major cities indicate an amazingly wide variety of cereal crops, fruits, sugarcane, cotton, and a few vegetables. Pastureland for goats and sheep is mentioned as being taxed more heavily than cropland as a means of deterring farmers from converting cropland into pastureland. The tax records indicate that date palms were untaxed because of the custom of travelers helping themselves to the dates that had fallen on the ground, yet Herodotus claims that they were taxed twice the rate of other crops because the palm provides food, wine, and a place for bees to make honey. Discrepancies such as this one leave modern historians in a quandary as to which is the more likely.

To increase crop yields in lands near rivers, irrigation was practiced. Ancient references to open trenches extending from a river to crops several miles away are common, but the most interesting comments describe qanats, or underground aqueducts. By running the water underground, very little evaporated, and food production did not suffer due to aboveground canals cutting across the land and reducing arable acreage.

On these farms labor was human, and the most useful tool was a farmer's hands. Planting was done by hand, either by poking a hole in the soil and inserting a single seed or by casting seeds by hand on soil and then hand-spreading topsoil over them. When the crops matured, especially grains, a sharp scythe cut the stalks. The grain was then separated from the stalks by beating it on the ground.

Craftspersons, both men and women, called kurtas, represented the second most common labor category. Ancient historians who saw them at work, and scribes who recorded their work on hundreds of clay tablets, attest to the large number of people who pursued some sort of craft. *Kurtas* were of two types: those who were free to work in their own villages for wages paid either in coins or by some sort of barter, and slaves who toiled for little more than food and clothing. The list of slave craftsmen working on the king's palaces and cities is lengthy, indicating tens of thousands who labored at hundreds of specialized crafts. The most commonly found entries in the cuneiform tablets mention rations of food distributed to sculptors, goldsmiths, shipbuilders, stonemasons, woodworkers, quarrymen, armor makers, weavers, and metalworkers. Entries further suggest that slave workers came from regions other than Persia, with Egypt accounting for more than any other satrapy.

Craftsmen generally were located in medium to large villages and cities because smaller settlements had too few residents to support them. They very often congregated according to the wares they made. Sections of cities often took their names from the goods sold there—potters' quarters, jewelry squares, barbers' tents, and cobblers' circles. Where craftspersons sold their goods was also where they produced them. Artisans worked at their trades, interrupting their work only to make a sale. Ancient visitors who left behind accounts of their travels in the Persian Empire commented on the sights, smells, and shouting of merchants hawking their wares and buyers complaining about the prices.

Funerals

Whatever someone in ancient Persia did for a living, retirement was a concept that did not exist. The only relief from hard labor was severe illness or death. And when death came, a variety of traditions determined that a variety of funeral rites would be practiced.

Funerals throughout the Persian Empire were solemn religious rituals. Most Persians in ancient times were followers of the Zoroastrian faith. They believed that a dead person's spirit would live on. Still, how the deceased person's body was treated mattered. Zoroastrianism prohibited either interment below ground or cremation. Instead, the most common practice was placing the body on the ground and covering it beneath a mound of dirt. On rare occasion, if the family was wealthier than most, a simple embalming of the body was performed before piling the earth upon it. Embalming involved removal of the blood followed by wrapping the body in a linen cloth sprinkled with spices such as clove and cinnamon. A form of embalming practiced by the Babylonians during the height of the Persian Empire was reported by Herodotus, who observed, "They bury their dead in honey, and have funeral lamentations like the Egyptians."[47]

Even in modern times, archaeologists occasionally discover undisturbed funeral mounds. Rarely, yet on occasion, the excavation yields a few objects placed next to the body. One of the more commonly found artifacts is simple jewelry, gold and silver rings, brooches, necklaces, and hair clips. Such items indicate a relatively well-off woman. Men, on the other had, were buried with weapons, generally one made of metal such as a dagger or a sword. Occasionally, more unusual items, such as a strigil—a metal scraper used to remove dirt from the body—or a ceramic oil lamp, are found.

In the top section of this relief carving, two Persian women in mourning follow closely behind a funerary chariot during a procession.

This Zoroastrian fire temple dates from the Achaemenid era. A sacred fire would have been kept burning in the temple at all times.

One of the more unusual funerary customs practiced in the region of the Persian plateau involved the practice of burying a person in an ossuary—a box containing just his or her bones. This in itself was not so unusual—other religions practice a similar custom—but what set the Persian tradition apart was the way in which the bones were separated from the flesh. According to Herodotus as well as Persian tablets, the dead person's body was placed on a mountain crag or desert depression and left there until wild dogs and birds of prey had eaten its flesh. Once the body was picked clean, the bones were placed in a box and buried.

Religion

Zoroastrianism, which was at the core of funeral rites, was a complex system of beliefs that directed people's behavior. According to tradition, Zoroaster was born in Persia in 628 B.C. When he was about thirty years old, he began traveling throughout Persia preaching a new religion that stressed prayer and accepted that both good and evil are separate entities constantly at war with each other. Prayer, Zoroaster taught, could increase the annual harvest, protect domestic animals, and help craftsmen whose handmade products played a major role in Persia's economy.

He believed that god took the form of Ormuzd—the embodiment of good and truth—as well as Ahriman—the incarnation of destruction and lies. Persians believed that a person had the freedom to choose between following Ormuzd or Ahriman. According to Zoroastrianism, following a person's death, the soul stood on a bridge where all good deeds were weighed against the bad ones. Then, the soul either fell from the bridge into a place of eternal agony or crossed the bridge to reach a place of pleasure.

Zoroastrianism was embraced by all the Persian kings beginning with Cyrus the

This wall shows a procession of Persian warriors. Beginning with the reign of Darius, military service became compulsory for Persian males.

Great. In a world where many peoples, such as the Egyptians and the Greeks, worshipped many gods, Zoroastrianism was unique in its promotion of monotheism.

Temples dedicated to Zoroaster were constructed throughout Persia. Only believers were allowed in the temples, where the most devout offered prayers, knelt by the sacred fire kept burning there, and consulted with priests known as Magi. Those who could not journey to a temple were supposed to offer private prayer, no matter where they were, at sunrise, noon, sunset, and midnight.

Persians took their beliefs with them into battle. As one of a handful of institutions that was common to many Persians, religion played a role in preparing soldiers for war. Zoroastrianism provided Persian fighting men with a hope that even after death another life would be awaiting them.

Military Service

Beginning with Darius the Great, Persian law decreed that all men serve in the military. Young men took their place in the army's ranks at the age of twenty. The law required service until they were fifty years old although, other than high-ranking officers, few remained on the battle line beyond their thirtieth birthday.

During the early years of the Persian Empire, all soldiers were Persian, but by the time of Cyrus the Great's death, Persians and non-Persians stood side by side on the battle line. Although large contingents of foot soldiers were drawn from local populations of each satrapy, military units manned by Persians were considered elite forces. These were the best-trained troops and the ones whose loyalty was beyond question. In addition to fighting wars in foreign countries, Persian troops acted as the king's bodyguard.

Exactly what job a young man was assigned in the Persian army was a function of social position. Men from prominent Persian families received choice commissions. As high-ranking officers, they received additional rewards in the form of land that they could sell at high profits in order to supplement the standard pay. The rank and file of the Persian army, however, the foot soldiers and the archers, came from the *skauthi*, the poor. This may have been a blessing to some parents who had many sons but little land to pass on to them as inheritance. Fathers were reluctant to divide their small plots of land among many sons, so the army was a convenient profession for young men with few prospects for an inheritance.

Poor though they may have been, all conscripts were required to provide their own equipment. In some cases young men without the money to purchase weapons and armor had to wait until their first battle and then take what they needed from a fallen comrade.

As burdensome as military service might be, the army was at the heart of the empire's existence and mandatory service a necessity. Without the idea of military service that was fostered in most young boys from an early age, the Persian army would never have achieved the high level of success it enjoyed for so many decades.

CHAPTER SIX

THE PERSIAN WAR MACHINE

The unprecedented rise of the Persian Empire in the span of little more than seventy years was first and foremost the result of a carefully organized military machine. Never before had leaders committed so much planning to their military deployments and composition of the army. Because of the broad sweep of the empire, soldiers had to be able to march great distances, overcome difficult terrain, sleep in makeshift camps, eat whatever they could scrounge, and be prepared for battle at a moment's notice. To accomplish such a difficult feat, the Persian military machine required careful planning and organization.

Cyrus Reforms the Military

One of Cyrus the Great's accomplishments was the reform of Persia's army. Following his initial successes on the battlefield, Cyrus understood the necessity of better organizing his army if he expected to continue his conquests. As his territory expanded and he encountered greater resistance from strong kings willing to fight to maintain their independence, Cyrus recognized the need for a standing army able to adapt quickly to different tactical circumstances.

This standing army, called the *spāda*, was divided into units of 150 warriors: 50 archers, 50 spearmen, and 50 horsemen. This grouping of three different types of warriors guaranteed that wherever they might be fighting, the unit's commander could rely on a variety of fighters trained in different skills to win the battle. Further flexibility was provided by organizing each basic unit of 50 warriors into ten 5-man squads, each of which was capable of fighting alone under the command of a corporal, called a *pascadasapati*, or several could be combined to form a larger detachment, called a *drafsha*. This organizational structure, based on the basic squad of 5 men, allowed the army to function as hundreds of well-trained, small groups fighting on their own, to combine with other squads to form a platoon, or to combine with many platoons to form a large massed force. No matter what sort of organization a general needed, he could quickly combine small units to create an entire army or decompose a large army into several smaller *drafshas*.

When assembled, a Persian force was a fearsome sight. Herodotus, who claims to have seen contingents of foot soldiers drawn up for battle, described their appearance:

> The Persians, who wore on their heads the soft hat called the tiara,

This artist's rendering depicts a Persian king (center) protected by his loyal guards, a spearman (left) and an archer.

and about their bodies, tunics with sleeves of diverse colors, having iron scales upon them like the scales of a fish. Their legs were protected by trousers; and they bore wicker shields for bucklers; their quivers hanging at their backs, and their arms being a short spear, a bow of uncommon size, and arrows of reed. They had likewise daggers suspended from their girdles along their right thighs.[48]

The Persian Battle Line

The way in which the various components of the Persian army were arranged before a battle was crucial to the outcome. The principal three elements of the army—the archers, infantrymen, and horsemen—were arrayed on the battlefield in such a way that each element could fight effectively without interfering with the actions of the other two.

The infantrymen represented the majority of the force and occupied the center of the front line of the army. These were the men who would bear the onslaught of the opposing army's charge. Cyrus placed his horsemen off to either flank so that when he gave them the order to charge, they would not trample their own comrades who were on foot. The archers took up position in the back, behind the foot soldiers.

The opening volley of battle was delivered by the archers at the same time the foot soldiers advanced toward the enemy formation. Archers were able to shoot their arrows from a distance of as much as 300 yards (274m); their objective was to rain down a torrent of arrows onto the opposing foot soldiers to disrupt their formation. Each Persian archer carried eighteen arrows, the number that could be accurately shot in three minutes. While arrows rained down on the enemy by the thousands, the infantry moved at a measured, quick pace, attempting to maintain an orderly line against an enemy whose ranks had been disrupted by arrows. Within 50 yards (46m) of the enemy front line, the foot soldiers threw their spears, drew their daggers, and plunged into the enemy's ranks to engage in hand-to-hand combat.

In the midst of this melee, the horsemen would charge. Using their horses as weapons, they waded into the bloody fray, overwhelming the enemy with a combination of trampling hooves and slashing swords. When the horsemen swept down upon them, foot soldiers were faced with the choice of fleeing, being trampled, or facing the swords wielded by the riders.

Not all accounts of the Persian battle line are consistent, however. In one account, reported by Herodotus, the archers were apparently shooting their arrows while positioned in front of the infantry, withdrawing through their ranks after firing their arrows to avoid hand-to-hand combat with the enemy. Yet a different account suggests that after they let loose with their volley of arrows, they grabbed shields and spears and joined the infantry in hand-to-hand combat.

The Role of the Chariot

Terrifying as hand-to-hand combat or a cavalry charge might be, nothing instilled fear like the appearance of chariots bearing down at full speed on foot soldiers. Ancient descriptions of Persian war chariots were of two types: those accommodating a driver and a warrior shooting arrows and hurling spears, and those with just one man performing both duties. Archaeologists have discovered decorative stone carvings of these chariots depicting them drawn by one, two, or four horses, depending on their size and weight. Xenophon describes war chariots that he saw this way:

> He [Cyrus] had chariots of war constructed with strong wheels. . . . The

box for the driver he constructed out of strong timbers in the form of a turret; and this rose in height to the drivers' elbows, so that they could manage the horses by reaching over the top of the box; and, besides, he covered the drivers with mail [chain-linked armor], all except their eyes. On both sides of the wheels, moreover, he attached to the axles steel scythes . . . this was so arranged with the intention of hurling the chariots into the midst of the enemy.[49]

Chariots could only be used if the battle took place on level, open ground since they

were apt to tip over or have wheels broken by rocks. Still, whether large or small, with whirling knives on their axles or not, when they were used chariots had a devastating effect on the morale of the opposing foot soldier. Both Herodotus and Xenophon describe battles in which the Persians employed three hundred, six hundred, or as many as one thousand chariots. Not even the most battle-tested veteran was likely to stand his ground against such a powerful onslaught. No implement of war was more feared than a chariot because of its speed and ability to run over soldiers, breaking their limbs, and throwing an entire phalanx into disarray. Even if foot soldiers could

avoid the horses' hooves and the chariot wheels, there was the additional danger of spears or arrows launched by the charioteer.

Persian Sea Power

The backbone of the Persian military machine was its army, yet its navy was also something to be reckoned with. When warships were needed, Persian kings typically relied upon their coastal allies who had long traditions of building and manning warships. The warship most commonly deployed by Persia was the trireme. This vessel was wooden, rarely longer than 125 feet (38m), and was propelled by three banks of thirty oars on each side of the ship. The 180 oarsmen worked in extremely confined spaces, with the lowest bank of rowers barely above the waterline while the highest bank sat about 12 feet (3.6m) above the water. The triremes were designed for short bursts of speed with an emphasis on maneuverability. But since they were top heavy they were rarely used in open water, where waves could easily capsize them. In addition to the rowers, each trireme carried a top-deck complement of about ten archers, ten spearmen, and another ten sailors or so whose jobs were to make repairs, cook, and command the ship.

Persian tactics for naval engagements, like all navies in ancient times, fell into three categories. The first was to row close enough to an enemy ship so the archers and spear throwers could hit their counterparts on deck. The second was to ram the enemy ship. Most triremes were fitted with a battering ram on the bow just below the waterline that was capable of smashing a hole in an enemy's hull. Following impact, the trireme's rowers would reverse their oar strokes to disengage the ram. The hole then would be left wide open, flooding and sinking the enemy ship. A third common tactic was to brush one's ship along the sides of an enemy ship and shear off all of its oars. Once the ship was disabled and floundering, it could be easily rammed and sunk.

Greek historians recorded many deaths following naval engagements. The cause of most deaths was not from spears and arrows, nor from men sinking in heavy armor, but

This scene from the Battle of Marathon shows the Persian battle line consisting of archers, cavalry, and spearmen arrayed before the charging Greeks.

rather because most troops, even though they were in the navy, could not swim.

Ancient historians report that strategies were drawn up the night before a naval battle. Fleets were organized into squadrons of five to ten ships each under the command of a captain who coordinated movements by waving a banner to signal each ship in his squadron. Often, a squadron set out in a column, and at a signal it clustered in a tight formation to ram enemy ships. As the battle was joined, archers and spearmen would fill the air with a shower of deadly missiles that could throw an organized fleet into chaos.

Persia's navy avoided the dangers of open water by sailing close to coastlines. This tactic had the secondary advantage of allowing for the provisioning of the fleet from a train of heavy wagons that closely followed on land as the fleet progressed along the coast. It

THE GREAT CHARIOT DEBATE

Xenophon's description of war chariots as having wheels bristling with spinning steel scythes has spurred debate among modern historians and archaeologists. Although such gruesome machines provoke the imagination, their existence is doubted by many scholars who have investigated their existence.

Xenophon's description of them is at odds with other ancient historians. Many of these historians saw war chariots, but none reported seeing the dramatic spinning steel blades. How would it be possible, skeptical modern historians ask, not to mention the scythes if indeed they existed? These skeptics further note the existence of several sculpted depictions of war chariots uncovered in Sardis and Persepolis that do not illustrate the spinning knives that Xenophon alleges he saw. Equally damaging to Xenophon's description is the existence of coinage from the late Persian Empire with representations of warriors driving chariots, yet none depicts the scythes on the wheels.

Without Xenophon's description, another picture of war chariots emerges. Some of the sculptured representations of war chariots depict very small chariots, little more than an axle, two wheels, and a simple platform on which stood one charioteer. This war chariot provided the charioteer no protection—contradicting Xenophon's description—yet its light weight would have increased its speed and maneuverability. Some historians believe that Xenophon mistakenly took the large, elaborate chariots used by kings in processionals for war chariots.

This carving depicts an ancient chariot drawing four warriors into battle.

was a standard practice for sailors to stop at night and draw their ships up on a beach so the crews could sleep and eat on land. This also gave the wood hulls of the ships time to dry and avoid becoming waterlogged.

As the fleet sailed the coastline, the army traveled inland on foot, in wagons, and with pack animals. Their life was tough because they often had to traverse long distances yet be fresh for battle at a moment's notice.

How the Persian Army Traveled

Moving a large army long distances along with their horses, weapons, and a myriad of battle paraphernalia was a severe test of discipline and planning. Yet the Persians proved capable of what even today would

be considered amazing feats of logistics. Several times in the relatively short history of the Persian Empire, armies numbering several tens of thousands marched long distances to the edges of the empire to do battle. Herodotus, in particular, makes this clear when he describes the logistics involved with Xerxes' invasion of Greece.

Herodotus, when calculating the size of the Persian army headed for Greece, claims, "What the exact number of the troops of each nation was I cannot say with certainty—for it is not mentioned by any one—but the whole land army together was found to amount to 1,700,000 men."[50] As a way of emphasizing the size of Xerxes' army, Herodotus later claimed it took seven days and seven nights for the entire force to cross the bridge the Persians had built to span the Hellespont. Contemporary historians dismiss such estimates, saying this is one of several cases where Herodotus, who had no military experience, grossly exaggerated the threat the Persians posed to the Greeks. Most modern historians estimate Xerxes' army at between fifty and one hundred thousand armed soldiers. Nonetheless, such a large contingent of warriors, and an equal number of support workers, including cooks, repairmen, engineers, hunters, and horse handlers, made for a huge undertaking to get everyone in place at the right time.

Such an enormous troop movement could hardly be kept secret or be undertaken without years of preparation. Herodotus reported that Xerxes sent diplomats throughout northern Greece offering friendship and gold to city-states that would guarantee safe passage for his troops. To ensure adequate food would be available for his troops passing through, Xerxes sent heralds months in advance of his army's arrival to arrange for large quantities of food in the villages along his route, as Herodotus explains:

> No sooner did the heralds who brought the orders give their message, than in every city the inhabitants made a division of their stores of corn [grain], and proceeded to grind flour of wheat and of barley for many months together. Besides this, they purchased the best cattle that they could find, and fattened them; and fed poultry and water-fowl in ponds and buildings, to be in readiness for the army.[51]

Soldiers marching long distances could not possibly be expected to carry the weight of full armor and weapons. Herodotus reports that Xerxes' army departed Sardis for Greece, a distance of about 750 miles (1,210km), and that the average distance his army covered in a day was 6 miles (10km) over the rough and treacherous terrain. To manage such a journey, the soldiers loaded their armor and weapons onto hundreds of wagons pulled by donkeys. The shields, of particular pride because many were made of wood covered with bronze and were inscribed with designs of personal significance, were placed in cotton sacks before being loaded on the wagons. This was done not only to prevent them from being scratched and dented but also, more importantly, to prevent sunlight from reflecting off of the shields and alerting the enemy of the army's approach.

Making Camp

At sunset the army stopped to rest, eat, feed the animals, and make repairs. Stopping for the night to make camp was a daunting undertaking for the Persian army. This was the case even though the troops slept in the open, without protection from tents. The camp experience for the king was very different from that of the rank-and-file soldier. According to Herodotus in his account of Xerxes' invasion of Greece, the king was the only man who had a tent set up for the night: "On the arrival of the Persians, a tent already pitched for the purpose of received Xerxes, who took his rest therein, while the soldiers remained under the open heaven."[52] The tent was placed as close to the center of the camp as possible for the safety of the king as well as for convenience. In the course of the evening, while the king was served dinner, the tent also served as the command center, and generals were frequently seen arriving to confer with the king while he ate his meal. Such conferences could be serious business. Xenophon tells the story of one king who summoned a general with whom he was particularly angry yet who was popular with his troops. Soldiers saw the general arrive at the king's tent but not depart. When morning came and the tent was disassembled and loaded on a wagon, the soldiers realized what had happened: Their general had been secretly executed and buried beneath the tent to avoid attracting the attention of his men.

Campsites were chosen for their defensible locations. Troop contingents traded the nightly responsibility of guarding the perimeter for the protection of everyone camping in the center. Night fighting was rare, but the enemy often sent spies to infiltrate the camp to determine the size and composition of the Persian force.

THE ARMY STANDARDS

Historians specializing in ancient Persian military tactics often wonder how commanders communicated with their units in the chaos of battle. A review of battles recorded by Greek historians mentions army standards—large colorful banners on poles—carried into battle and used for communications between commanders and their units. Corroborating the historians are low-relief sculptures at Persepolis that depict standard bearers carrying ornately decorated banners in the midst of their units.

Modern historians explain that army standards were brightly colored visual markers employed to show the position of units and to distinguish one unit from all others. Visible over the heads of the troops, standards could be used to mark rallying or deployment points or to signal the direction soldiers in a particular unit should move. Xenophon describes the king's standard as being decorated with a gold eagle in the *Anabasis*: "The royal standard, a kind of golden eagle, with wings extended, perched on a bar of wood, and raised upon a lance."

Bearing the standard into battle was considered an honor, as Xenophon indicates in the *Anabasis*, saying that the soldier who threw the spear that killed Cyrus the Younger at the Battle of Cunaxa was awarded "the privilege of carrying ever after a golden cock standard upon his spear before the first ranks of the army in all expeditions."

Once the camp was established, the food wagons came forward while fires for cooking were lit. Butchers had the responsibility of slaughtering cattle, chickens, and whatever other animals could be found to feed the troops. Bread, which took a long time to bake, was usually procured from villages along the route and was usually paid for to avoid anger-

BRIDGING THE HELLESPONT

Few ancient engineering feats rival that of the pontoon bridge that Xerxes ordered constructed across the Hellespont. Permanent stone bridges could not be built at that time because concrete had not yet been discovered. Instead, crossing rivers and straits required floating pontoon bridges.

Herodotus provides the most precise technical details of how this pontoon bridge was built. He tells us that Xerxes demanded two bridges to be built, each consisting of 676 warships lashed together side by side by ropes over which troops, horses, and carts could travel without touching water. When all this was completed, the ropes were drawn taut from the shore by the help of wooden capstans, wheels turned by hand. The boat decks were then covered with a variety of materials to simulate a road, as Herodotus describes in his history *The Persian Wars*:

> "When the bridge across the channel was thus complete, trunks of trees were sawn into planks, which were cut to the width of the bridge, and these were laid side by side upon the tightened cables, and then fastened on the top. This done, brushwood was brought, and arranged upon the planks, after which earth was heaped upon the brushwood, and the whole trodden down into a solid mass. Lastly a bulwark was set up on either side of this causeway, of such a height as to prevent the horses from seeing over it and taking fright at the water."

King Xerxes managed to cross the Hellespont by lashing warships together to form a pontoon bridge, as this woodcut shows.

ing the native population. Following dinner, the men pulled blankets and animal skins from the supply wagons and slept with their weapons until the morning horn was sounded.

Military Engineers

As the army advanced, the rough, roadless terrain required the skilled work of military engineers to prepare the way. Moving the Persian military machine required careful planning on the part of civil engineers to ensure the presence and adequacy of roads, bridges, canals, and whatever else the army might need. During the time when the Persian Empire was at its height, its military engineers accomplished feats that were remarkable even by today's standards.

One of the most labor-intensive engineering feats was the canal that Persian engineers dug at Mount Athos prior to Xerxes' invasion of Greece in 480 B.C. Xerxes ordered it dug through a peninsula so that his fleet could avoid sailing through the treacherous waters around it, where hundreds of ships were known to have sunk and where the Persian fleet had run into trouble thirteen years earlier. On the king's orders, engineers and their work crews cut a canal 3 miles (5km) long, wide enough so that two triremes could row through it side by side—roughly 100 feet (30m)—and about 30 feet (9m) deep. Herodotus provides this description:

> Now the manner in which they dug was the following: a line was drawn across by the city of Sane; and along this the various nations parceled out among themselves the work to be done. When the trench grew deep, the workmen at the bottom continued to dig, while others handed the earth, as it was dug out, to laborers placed higher up upon ladders, and these taking it, passed it on farther, till it came at last to those at the top, who carried it off and emptied it away.[53]

In spite of Herodotus's description of this canal, many modern historians questioned its existence. They performed some rough calculations and concluded that such a trench would have required the removal of roughly 2 million cubic yards (1.5 million cu. m) of earth, which, they speculated, would have taken thousands of men at least one hundred years to complete. Yet in the 1960s, technicians taking aerial photographs over Mount Athos developed their film to find an inexplicable band of earth across the peninsula that was slightly different from nearby soils. When this anomaly became known, archaeologists flocked to the area. Their excavations confirmed the existence of a canal dating to the time of the Persian invasion. Archaeologists initially found that the earth in the band was slightly less compact than the surrounding earth, and once excavations were under way, rudimentary metal digging tools were found along with a cache of hundreds of gold coins dating to that time that confirmed Herodotus's story.

In spite of the remarkable work of all who contributed to the success of the Persian war machine, the empire was not destined to last for long. For a variety of reasons, it began to lose cohesiveness following Xerxes' defeat at the hands of the Greeks, and it never recovered. The decline could not have been seen at the time because the loss to Greece was negligible to the great Persian Empire in terms of costing it territory and wealth. Instead, the cause of decline was from within.

CHAPTER SEVEN

COLLAPSE AND DEFEAT

Following the death of Xerxes in 465 B.C., no great leader stepped forward to take up the banner of the empire and move it forward. A combination of weak rulers from outside the Achaemenid dynasty, palace intrigue, personal greed, and inept military leaders left the empire vulnerable to attack even as it withered from within. One hundred years after Xerxes' death, the Persian Empire's great wealth and its growing weakness made it a tempting target for would-be conquerors.

Outrage in the Court

The promise of Xerxes' earlier years as a leader equal to Cyrus and Darius remained unfulfilled. Although the empire remained secure and well administered, Xerxes' failure to secure additional territory, and especially his failure to conquer Greece, triggered palace intrigues among his nobles. High-ranking bureaucrats blamed generals for the defeat and retreat, and generals blamed bureaucrats. Suspicions swept through Sardis, where Xerxes worked to administer the empire, causing many to speculate about whose heads would be severed as signs of who were to blame.

In the midst of this turmoil, Xerxes made the situation worse by making amorous advances toward his brother's wife. When she refused his attentions, Xerxes tried to intimidate her by forcing the marriage of her daughter, Artayntes, to his eldest son, Darius. Xerxes then managed to make the situation even worse by switching his attention to Artayntes—who was now his daughter-in-law. The queen, thinking that Artayntes' mother was involved, ordered the woman to be horribly mutilated. A few days later, as Artayntes and her entire family tried to flee, all were overtaken by soldiers and executed.

Increasingly isolated and fearful of palace intrigues, Xerxes ordered a series of executions within the extended family. At this point, he could trust only Artabanos, the commander of his bodyguard, and Aspamithres, his most trusted eunuch. Rumors of the problems at the court spread. Revolts among cities that had previously been loyal to the king flared. The Greek cities along the Ionian coast revolted, as did others that sensed the vulnerability of the empire. Xerxes sent a fleet and army against the rebellious cities only to see both contingents crushed. Once other non-Persian tribes saw the success of the Greeks, they hurried to join with them against Xerxes.

Xerxes retreated inland to spend his time overseeing the building of the palace complex at Persepolis. Unlike his predecessors Cyrus and Darius, both of whom expended their energies to their dying days adding territory and wealth to the empire, Xerxes seemed content to enter into a period of retreat and retirement rather than conquest.

Retirement did not, in the end, keep Xerxes safe. In August 465 B.C. Xerxes was stabbed to death in his sleep by a group of conspirators headed by Artabanos, with the assistance of the king's trusted eunuch, Aspamithres.

Murder in the Palace

Murder within the royal family did not end with Xerxes. Before anyone could react to his death, Artabanos set in motion more murder and intrigue. He picked Xerxes'

younger son, Artaxerxes, to be the next king, but not before Artaxerxes was told to murder his older brother, Darius, which he did. For a short time Artaxerxes ruled under the control of Artabanos, but the youth's rule was not to Artabanos's liking. In 464 B.C. Artabanos set upon Artaxerxes with a sword, and as he was in the act of attempting to kill the young king, he himself was slain by a fellow conspirator.

Wounded but not fatally, Artaxerxes recovered from this attempt on his life and remained on the throne. His position was seen to be precarious, however, and powerful families in the Egyptian satrapy saw his weakness as an invitation to revolt. Egypt, as had been the case with all satrapies, had continued to pay a fortune in tribute to the

These ruins are all that remain of Persepolis, the glorious seat of the Persian Empire. With the death of Xerxes, the empire was plunged into chaos.

This artist's rendering shows the grandeur of Xerxes' palace at Persepolis, where conspirators stabbed the ruler to death in his sleep.

Persian king, and it had received little in return. In 460 B.C., therefore, the Egyptians gathered a mercenary army and, with the assistance of a Greek fleet that had sailed to their defense, rose up against Artaxerxes.

The Greek fleet reached Egypt but failed to overpower the fleet sent by Artaxerxes. In 456 B.C. Artaxerxes selected a capable general, Megabyzos, to quell the revolt. Following a lengthy series of battles, Megabyzos forced the Egyptians to surrender. Their leaders were then taken to Susa, where Artaxerxes executed them. Despite the end of the Egyptian rebellion, Artaxerxes had to remain on guard. His victory, unlike those of his predecessors, had been the work of Megabyzos, not his own military genius.

Although the remainder of Artaxerxes' rule was relatively calm, historian J.M. Cook makes the point that "the lull in the second half of Artaxerxes I's reign does not necessarily imply firm rule—a gradual weakening of Persian control of the more distant parts of the empire would have been unlikely to have filtered through [to Greek historians]."[54] Furthermore, and perhaps more telling of Artaxerxes' tenuous position, Megabyzos revolted against him sometime around 448 B.C. and defeated the king's army in two battles. However, following a truce and an agreement, Artaxerxes allowed Megabyzos and his family to return to Syria as a satrap; this would have been a highly improbable outcome had it occurred under any of Artaxerxes' stronger predecessors.

Brother at the Throat of Brother

In 424 B.C. Artaxerxes died, once again throwing the empire into chaos. Artaxerxes' one legitimate son, Xerxes II, stepped forward and assumed the throne; but within one month, he was murdered in his sleep. The assassin was one of the sons of Artaxerxes by a concubine, but he too was soon murdered by yet another illegitimate son, who then raised an army to enforce his hold on power and took the name Darius II.

Under Darius II, the condition of the empire worsened. He was forced to contend with one revolt after another that further weakened the empire. Around 415 B.C. he suppressed a revolt among the Medes and then another among the Egyptians. During the uncertainty caused by the revolts, one of his personal bodyguards, a eunuch, plotted to make himself king. Darius II had the would-be usurper executed, but rebellions within the empire continued. By the time

Darius II died in 404 B.C. Egypt had revolted and was forever lost to the Persian Empire.

With the death of Darius II, yet another wave of palace murder ensued. Darius II had chosen his oldest son, Artaxerxes II, to succeed him, but once the king died, the situation changed, Darius II's widow, Parysatis, favored her younger son, Cyrus III, as ruler.

Parysatis did not get her way. The morning Artaxerxes II's coronation ceremony was scheduled to take place, a plot by Cyrus III to kill him was uncovered. Artaxerxes II ordered his brother to be killed, but Parysatis dramatically threw herself on her oldest son, pleading with Artaxerxes II to spare his brother's life. Moved by his mother's tears, the new king spared Cyrus III, made him a satrap in Anatolia (modern Turkey), and sent him away.

Artaxerxes II soon regretted that moment of mercy. Cyrus III recruited a combined Greek and Persian army to march against his brother. In hopes of keeping his plot a secret and concealing his army, he continued to pay annual tribute to his brother. But Artaxerxes II got wind of the plot and prepared for a decisive battle.

In 401 B.C. the two brothers faced each other at Cunaxa, near Babylon, backed by armies that numbered between ten and thirteen thousand men each. Historians know a great deal about this battle because the historian Xenophon, who fought there on the side of Cyrus III, made an account of the event. Xenophon describes the clash of the armies and the final moment when the two brothers fought each other:

> He [Cyrus III] caught sight of the King and the compact body [of soldiers]

DRAMA AT CUNAXA

The Greek historian Xenophon provides an eyewitness account of the Battle of Cunaxa. Xenophon was a seasoned fighter who provided the following dramatic account of the battle in his book the *Anabasis:*

> It was midday, and the enemy were not yet in sight; but when afternoon was coming on, there was seen a rising dust, which appeared at first like a white cloud, but some time later like a kind of blackness in the plain, extending over a great distance.
>
> As the enemy came nearer and nearer, there were presently flashes of bronze here and there, and spears and the hostile ranks began to come into sight. There were horsemen in white cuirasses [chest armor] on the left wing of the enemy; next to them were troops with wicker shields and, farther on, hoplites [infantrymen] with wooden shields which reached to their feet, these latter being Egyptians, people said; and then more horsemen and more bowmen.
>
> All these troops were marching in national divisions, each nation in a solid square. In front of them were the so-called scythe-bearing chariots, at some distance from one another; and the scythes they carried reached out sideways from axles and were also set under the chariot bodies, pointing towards the ground, so as to cut to pieces whatever they met; the intention, then, was that they should drive into the ranks of the Greeks and cut the troops to pieces.

The armies of Artaxerxes II and Cyrus III clash at the Battle of Cunaxa in 401 B.C.

around him; and on the instant he lost control of himself and, with the cry "I see the man," rushed upon him and struck him in the breast and wounded him through his breastplate. . . . While Cyrus was delivering his stroke, however, some one hit him a hard blow under the eye with a javelin; and then followed a struggle between the King and Cyrus and the attendants who supported each of them. . . . So died Cyrus.[55]

Artaxerxes II survived his brother's revolt, but he did not survive as well throughout his empire. As had been the case since Xerxes' defeat at the hands of the Greeks, the king was forced to deal with one revolt after another.

A Crippled Empire

Artaxerxes II was forced to rely on means other than his own army to keep the empire alive and tribute pouring in. Although Egypt had been lost, the king attempted to rein in other rebellious satrapies with mercenary troops paid to fight alongside the Persian forces. Although they were effective at times, mercenaries were unreliable. They had a tendency to retreat when the going got tough rather than stand and fight. And since they fought for money, mercenaries were constantly threatening to go home if their wages were not increased. When mercenary armies failed, Artaxerxes resorted to bribery. On more than one occasion, the king simply scooped thousands of gold coins into bags and delivered them to rebel leaders in exchange for their surrender on the battlefield.

This painting depicts Artaxerxes II in hand-to-hand combat with his brother Cyrus III at Cunaxa.

When Artaxerxes II died in 358 B.C., his son, Artaxerxes III, inherited an empire weakened and fragmented in a way that would have been unimaginable to earlier Achaemenid kings. Although his forebears might have applauded his attempts to hold the empire together, the intrigues within the palace continued unchecked. The regicide continued. Artaxerxes III was slain by his most trusted eunuch, Bagoas, who installed one of the king's sons. The eunuch murdered that unlucky heir and replaced him with Darius III, who then turned on Bagoas and killed him.

Macedonian Revenge

The internal collapse exemplified by this spate of murders within the palace, a growing dependence on unreliable mercenary armies, a rising reliance on bribery, and increasing disaffection among subject peoples made the Persian Empire a target for other rulers interested in expanding their own realms. Just north of Greece in Macedonia, King Philip had designs on creating his own empire.

In 338 B.C. Philip started expanding his boundaries by defeating a combined Greek army of prominent city-states in central Greece at the Battle of Chaeronea. Having subdued all of Greece, an objective that had escaped both Darius and Xerxes, he turned his gaze toward the floundering Persian Empire.

Philip had reason to yearn to invade Persia. Several generations earlier, both Darius and Xerxes had subdued Macedonia in preparation for attempting to conquer Greece. Philip claimed his interest in invading Persia was to avenge these earlier Persian invasions of his homeland. In the spring of 336 B.C. Philip began the invasion of Persia. He sent his generals with a force of ten thousand troops to cross over into Anatolia in advance of the main army. But about this time Philip was assassinated by a disgruntled Macedonian nobleman.

Philip's death set the stage for the rise of his eighteen-year-old son, Alexander. In 334 B.C. the young king assembled a combined force of forty thousand foot soldiers and horsemen and crossed the Hellespont at the exact spot where Xerxes' army had crossed in the opposite direction 146 years before. In spite of his youth, Alexander possessed remarkable confidence in his ability to defeat an army of Persians and Greek mercenaries. At the first battle between the two powers, Alexander displayed his tactical skills by defeating the opposing army and then his personality by displaying compassion for the vanquished Persians by allowing them to return home. (He was less merciful toward the Greek mercenaries, slaughtering every one of them.)

Darius III, shocked by Alexander's stunning success, hastily assembled another army and awaited Alexander at Issus, a coastal city at the extreme northeastern corner of the Mediterranean. In 333 B.C. at Issus, Alexander's army drew up facing Darius's force. Following a full day of carnage on both sides, Alexander's troops broke through the Persian line, forcing Darius III to flee for his life, leaving behind his mother, wife, and children. When Alexander learned that his generals had captured the Persian king's entire family, he magnanimously set them free. Following Alexander's decisive victory at Issus, a string of Persian cities along the eastern Mediterranean coast surrendered to Alexander. When the young commander worked his way south to Egypt, he was given a hero's welcome by the Egyptians, who had long hated their Persian oppressors.

Darius III recognized the gravity of his predicament. Never in the history of the Persian Empire had a foreign army penetrated the heart of the empire in a series of victories over Persian forces. Darius III was in need of a drastic reversal of fortune to survive.

XENOPHON

Born in Athens sometime between 431 and 427 B.C., Xenophon was one of the great Greek historians. The son of a wealthy Athenian, Xenophon studied under the greatest philosopher and teacher of his time, Socrates. Following in the footsteps of Herodotus, he traveled to Persia and reported on the kings, life in the Persian Empire, and the role that Greek armies played as the empire began to flounder.

Xenophon learned to report accurately about the military as a soldier. He began as a cavalryman fighting for Athens sometime around 409 B.C. and later left Athens in 401 to fight with a mercenary Greek army in Persia supporting Cyrus III against King Artaxerxes II at the Battle of Cunaxa. Following Cyrus's defeat and death, Xenophon wrote his great history of the war, the *Anabasis*, chronicling life in Persia and the wars in which he fought. He later wrote other works about Persian history, including *Cyrus*, in which he provides a detailed biography of Cyrus the Great. The descriptions and insights that Xenophon provides about the Persian Empire, warfare, and armies rank him as one of the greatest Greek historians.

A painting portrays Xenophon and his fellow Greek mercenaries reaching the Black Sea after being routed at Cunaxa.

The Last Battle

Darius III sued for peace, offering Alexander half his empire if he would go no further. Alexander, however, having won every battle against Persian armies, scoffed at such an offer. He then demonstrated his supremacy by boldly crossing the Euphrates and Tigris rivers unopposed.

Seeing his empire fall one satrapy after another, and nursing his wounded pride following Alexander's refusal to accept his peace offer, Darius III had no choice but to gamble his entire empire at one grand, final battle. In 331 B.C., 180 miles (290 km) north of Babylon and just east of the Tigris River, the two kings and their armies met. Darius ordered his men to clear a broad plain of all trees and rocks because he planned to deploy his chariots. Alexander, on the other hand, rested his army for several days and fed them well. Then, when he was ready, Alexander moved toward Darius's position,

A Roman mosaic depicts Alexander's victory over Darius III at Issus in 333 B.C. The victory spelled doom for the Persian Empire.

beginning to fly when he came on the scene of conflict; so that again he wheeled, and started in pursuit of Darius once more, keeping up the chase while daylight lasted. [The next morning] Darius went on fleeing without any rest. However, the money and all his other wealth were captured, likewise his chariot; and his spear and bow were also taken, as they had been after Issus.[56]

Alexander then systematically captured all major Persian cities, beginning with Babylon, Susa, and the crown jewel of the Persian Empire, Persepolis. Alexander captured great treasure at Persepolis, and after carting it away, he burned the city to the ground. Some ancient historians claimed he destroyed it as a grand gesture signaling the end of the Persian Empire, others claim he did so as revenge for the destruction of Athens by Xerxes 149 years earlier.

By 330 B.C. Darius III had died and no member of the Achaemenid dynasty remained to rule. Alexander solidified his grip on the empire by marrying the daughter of Darius III. He also, in keeping with the wisdom of Cyrus the Great and Darius, gained the respect of the Persians by treating the Persians and the Macedonians equally. He allowed Persians to serve in his army and provided Greek teachers to educate Persian nobles' children. For the next seven years, until his death in 323 B.C., Alexander remained in Persia. Following Alexander's

and the next morning he attacked in battle formation. As was the case at Issus, Alexander outmaneuvered Darius III, forcing him to flee. The Greek historian Arrian recorded the final moments of the battle:

Meantime the Thessalian cavalry in a splendid struggle were not falling short of Alexander's own success in the combat. For the Barbarians [Persians] on the right wing were already

THE UNUSUAL LIFE
OF ALEXANDER THE GREAT

Alexander the Great, although principally known as the conqueror of the Persian Empire, lived a most atypical life. A man of considerable complexity, he was born in Macedonia in 356 B.C. His father, King Philip, taught him that he was a descendant of Achilles, the great mythical warrior of the Trojan wars. From the earliest age, Alexander was expected to be a great warrior and king.

When Alexander was thirteen years old, he became the student of the great Greek philosopher Aristotle. Aristotle stimulated Alexander's interest in reading and learning. Under Aristotle's care, the boy gained an interest in philosophy, medicine, and science. At just sixteen, Alexander was summoned to suppress a rebellion while his father was away. Alexander crushed the rebellion, attacked the rebels' stronghold, and renamed it Alexandropoulos, meaning "the City of Alexander," after himself.

Part of Alexander's unusual character was his violent temper. As a young man, Alexander had a violent relationship with his father. At a feast to celebrate his father's recent marriage, the two argued and a brawl ensued. Philip pulled his sword, lunged at Alexander, but stumbled over a couch and fell to the floor. Alexander then sneered at his father and mocked him, saying that although he was about to invade Persia, he was incapable of moving from one couch to another.

Alexander could be both mystical and practical. He prayed to a variety of gods, but he also planned brilliant military strategies and paid attention to the details of supply and logistics while preparing for battle. His soldiers adored him, as did most who met him, yet he was also capable of executing thousands of people who stood in his way of conquest.

Alexander the Great is known to posterity as the conqueror who brought an end to the Persian Empire.

death, the immense Persian Empire was divided among his generals, never to regain its dominant position. No member of the Achaemenid family stepped forth to recapture what Alexander had seized. The decline of the Persian Empire had begun before Darius III, but it was, nonetheless, just as dramatic and rapid as had been the empire's ascent two hundred years earlier.

During the empire's roughly 220 years a succession of noteworthy Persian kings developed brilliant stratagems for empire building while later kings, of decidedly inferior ability, foolishly squandered away all that their predecessors had achieved. This was not an unusual phenomenon, as professor Tom B. Jones points out in his book *Ancient Civilization*, "It is not uncommon in ancient empires to see the founder, and on occasion a few successors, as the empire's architects. They are the ones who defined the empire, understood its operation, and knew how to preserve it. Those that follow rarely fare as well."[57]

Fortunately, however, archaeologists have been successful in excavating much of what was once emblematic of that mighty empire, and students today can easily visualize and understand the exceptional empire built by those early Persian kings.

A RICH AND SHARED HERITAGE

Citizens of modern-day Iraq and Iran can legitimately claim cultural ties to ancient Persia. For centuries, peoples of both nations have taken pride in tracing their histories back twenty-five hundred years. Books and Web sites representing the two nations make references to Cyrus the Great, ancient Persian traditions (some still practiced) recorded on cuneiform tablets, and the ancient history that involves both countries.

Beginning around the early twentieth century, both countries began independent campaigns to gather as many excavated artifacts as they could find and display them in museums in a handful of major cities. Foreign archaeologists were welcomed to assist because of their experience and financial backing from major universities and government grants. By the mid–twentieth century, museum collections in both countries grew and rivaled many better-known collections of Greek and Egyptian artifacts.

Internationally Acclaimed Collections

The major collections of ancient Persian art located in the capital cities of Baghdad and Tehran have long dazzled local residents as well as foreign visitors and scholars. At the National Museum of Antiquities in Baghdad, 170,000 rare artifacts were on display. Choice items included cuneiform texts that are the oldest known examples of poems and mathematical treatises and historical accounts. There is also a large collection of ornate alabaster vases and stone carvings dating to the time of Cyrus the Great and gold drinking cups dating to the end of the empire.

In Tehran, the Archaeological Museum houses a collection of artifacts dating back to Cyrus the Great. Most revered is a majestic statue of Darius the Great removed from the palace gatehouse at Susa. It is the first known large-scale statue in the round from the Achaemenid period. The museum also houses an exhibit of ancient clay pots, cuneiform tablets, and rare bronzes statues. A sixth-century B.C. stone winged lion from Susa and a relief of Darius the Great recovered from the treasury at Persepolis also are found in the museum.

While these collections were being accumulated, however, political and religious tensions between the two nations grew, causing each nation to spend increasing amounts of money on war preparation and less on collecting and displaying their shared heritage.

Fragile Riches

In 1980 the vulnerability of ancient artifacts to war's devastation was demonstrated when the tensions between Iran and Iraq triggered a war that lasted ten years. A few archaeological sites in both countries were destroyed, and some artifacts were stolen from museums. During the Iran-Iraq War, more ancient artifacts had been destroyed than had been discovered during the previous three decades. At the war's end, museum curators pleaded for the return of stolen objects and invited foreign archaeologists, who had fled at the beginning of hostilities, to return.

In the years following the war, both countries worked to rebuild their collections and better protect their shared cultural heritage. Scholars working in the major archaeological museums in the capital cities of Baghdad and Tehran modernized them in hopes of better preserving the irreplaceable collections in each country. Much remains to be done, however. Particularly following the American-led invasion of Iraq in May 2003, the National Museum of Antiquities in Baghdad suffered enormous losses to looters. Many priceless objects dating back to before the rise of ancient Persia were lost. Only time will tell whether humankind can recover this portion of the story of this ancient civilization.

NOTES

Introduction:
The World's First Great Empire

1. A.T. Olmstead, *History of the Persian Empire.* Chicago: University of Chicago Press, 1948, p. xiii.
2. Olmstead, *History of the Persian Empire*, p. viii.
3. Olmstead, *History of the Persian Empire*, p. viii.

Chapter 1: Persia Before the Empire

4. George Grote, "Conquests of Cyrus the Great," *History World International*, http://history-world.org/persians2.htm.
5. Diodorus Siculus, *Library of History*, trans. C.H. Oldfather, vol. 2. Cambridge, MA: Loeb Classical Library, 1954, p. 147.
6. Quoted in Farsinet, "Cyrus Charter of Human Rights Cylinder." www.farsinet.com/cyrus.

Chapter 2: Masters of the Persian Empire

7. Herodotus, *Persian Wars*, trans. George Rawlinson. New York: Modern Library, 1942, p. 72.
8. Herodotus, *Persian Wars*, p. 43.
9. Herodotus, *Persian Wars*, p. 44.
10. Quoted in A.R. Burn, *Persia and the Greeks: The Defense of the West, c. 546–478* B.C. New York: St. Martin's, 1962, p. 61.
11. Xenophon, *Cyrus*, trans. H.G. Dakyns. London: J.M. Dent & Sons, 1914, p. 251.
12. Quoted in Burn, *Persia and the Greeks*, p. 96.
13. Herodotus, *Persian Wars*, p. 423.
14. Herodotus, *Persian Wars*, p. 479.
15. Herodotus, *Persian Wars*, p. 493.
16. Herodotus, *Persian Wars*, p. 493.

Chapter 3: A Genius for Administration

17. Jim Hicks, *The Persians.* New York: Time-Life, 1975, p. 101.
18. Quoted in Herodotus, *Persian Wars*, p. 273.
19. J.M. Cook, *The Persian Empire.* New York: Schocken, 1983, pp. 40–41.
20. Richard Frye, *The Heritage of Persia.* Cleveland: World, 1963, pp. 10–11.
21. Herodotus, *Persian Wars*, p. 194.
22. Herodotus, *Persian Wars*, pp. 257–58.
23. Herodotus, *Persian Wars*, p. 260.
24. Xenophon, *Anabasis*, trans. Carleton L. Brownson. Cambridge, MA: Harvard University Press, 1961, p. 18.
25. Herodotus, *Persian Wars*, p. 633.

26. Herodotus, *Persian Wars*, p. 633.

Chapter 4:
Life at the Court of the Great Kings

27. Herodotus, *Persian Wars*, pp. 514–15.

28. Quoted in Pierre Briant, *From Cyrus to Alexander: A History of the Persian Empire*, trans. Peter T. Daniels. Winona Lake, IN: Eisenbrauns, 2002, p. 221.

29. Herodotus, *Persian Wars*, p. 520.

30. Xenophon, *Anabasis*, p. 5.

31. Xenophon, *Cyrus*, p. 93.

32. Herodotus, *Persian Wars*, p. 696.

33. Herodotus, *Persian Wars*, p. 443.

34. Quoted in Briant, *From Cyrus to Alexander*, p. 277.

35. Cook, *The Persian Empire*, p. 135.

36. Quoted in Briant, *From Cyrus to Alexander*, p. 273.

37. Xenophon, *Cyrus*, p. 244.

38. Quoted in Briant, *From Cyrus to Alexander*, p. 270.

Chapter 5:
Everyday Life in the Persian Empire

39. Xenophon, *Hellenica*, trans. Carleton L. Brownson. Cambridge, MA: Harvard University Press, 1968, p. 237.

40. Xenophon, *Cyrus*, p. 221.

41. Quoted in Briant, *From Cyrus to Alexander*, p. 123.

42. Quoted in Briant, *From Cyrus to Alexander*, p. 123.

43. Quoted in Briant, *From Cyrus to Alexander*, p. 60.

44. Xenophon, *Cyrus*, p. 10.

45. Herodotus, *Persian Wars*, p. 76.

46. Strabo, *Geography of Strabo*, trans. H.L. Jones. Cambridge, MA: Loeb Classical Library, 1954, p. 127.

47. Herodotus, *Persian Wars*, p. 107.

Chapter 6: The Persian War Machine

48. Herodotus, *Persian Wars*, p. 523.

49. Xenophon, *Cyrus*, p. 193.

50. Herodotus, *Persian Wars*, p. 522.

51. Herodotus, *Persian Wars*, pp. 540–41.

52. Herodotus, *Persian Wars*, p. 541.

53. Herodotus, *Persian Wars*, pp. 507–508.

Chapter 7: Collapse and Defeat

54. Cook, *The Persian Empire*, p. 128.

55. Xenophon, *Anabasis*, pp. 30–31.

56. Quoted in *Eye Witness to History*, "Alexander Defeats the Persians, 331 B.C.," 2000. www.eyewitnesstohistory. com/alexander.htm.

57. Tom B. Jones, *Ancient Civilization*. Chicago: Rand McNally, 1960, p. 433.

FOR FURTHER READING

Books

J.M. Cook, The *Persian Empire*. New York: Schocken, 1983. Cook's comprehensive book on the Persian Empire emphasizes Persian political and military history yet also includes chapters on religion, art, and social customs. Maps and illustrations make the book suitable for students.

J.E. Curtice, *Forgotten Empire: The World of Ancient Persia*. Berkeley and Los Angeles: University of California Press, 2005. This work is primarily a collection of beautiful photographs detailing an exhibit on display at the British Museum in London of archaeological finds from the royal Persian palaces at Persepolis and Susa.

Jim Hicks, *The Persians*. New York: Time-Life, 1975. This is an excellent history of the Persian Empire written for the student audience. It is thorough and provides maps and photographs of Persian art and architecture.

Harold Lamb, *Cyrus the Great*. Garden City, New York: Doubleday, 1960. Lamb is a renowned historian who presents a historical novel about the great Persian king. The book is factually accurate and is presented in a style that highlights Cyrus's importance to the history of the Persian Empire.

Marie Neurath, *They Lived Like This in Ancient Persia*. London: Franklin Watts, 1970. This book written for young adults provides accurate insights into the everyday life of ancient Persia. Its chapters cover topics about ancient Persian society such as family life, clothing, homes, education, marriage, village life, and religion.

Amini Sam, *Pictorial History of Iran: Ancient Persia Before Islam, 15000 B.C.–625 A.D.* London: Lightning Source, 2001. This book provides short, easy-to-read essays and ample photographs depicting the history of Iran. The final four chapters cover the Persian Empire up to the beginning of Islam in the seventh century A.D.

Philip de Souza, *The Greek and Persian Wars, 499–386* B.C. Oxford, England: Osprey, 2003. This book covers events leading up to the Persian wars against Greece, details of the battles, and the aftermath of the Greek victory. The author amply cites Herodotus, recent archaeological evidence, and theories of modern historians. This is an excellent book for junior and senior high school readers.

John Warry, *Alexander, 334–323* B.C.: *Conquest of the Persian Empire*. Oxford, England: Osprey, 1991. This book, which covers Alexander's conquest of Persia, is excellent for young readers. The text is amply supplemented by color maps, drawings, art photographs, and photographs of archaeological sites.

Web Sites

Antiquity (www.antiquity.ac.uk). This is the Web site for *Antiquity* magazine, which is published quarterly. The Web site provides the latest archaeological research in dozens of countries throughout the world. Although access to complete articles requires a membership, shortened versions are available for free.

Archaeological Resource Guide for Europe (http://odur.let.rug.nl/ arge). This site allows students to access archaeological information about Europe and the Middle East either by country or by historical period.

Archaeology Magazine (www.archaeology.org). *Archaeology Magazine* provides a Web site that offers many of the articles carried in its magazine. Its featured articles, many of which present recent findings in Iran and Iraq, are suited for students and provide color photographs and maps.

Public Broadcasting Service (www.pbs.org). The Public Broadcasting Service Web site is an excellent resource for students researching topics about ancient Persia. Articles include a broad spectrum of Persian history as well as the impact of recent wars on ancient Persian archaeological sites.

Smithsonian (www.si.edu). The Smithsonian site, under the heading "Archaeology and Ancient Cultures," provides dozens of links to archaeological excavations taking place in Iran and Iraq that discuss finds from ancient Persia. Most articles are written for the young-adult audience.

Works Consulted

Books

Pierre Briant, *From Cyrus to Alexander: A History of the Persian Empire*. Trans. Peter T. Daniels. Winona Lake, IN: Eisenbrauns, 2002. This is the most respected and most comprehensive book on the Persian Empire. It is well organized, well documented, and contains several different indexes for quick referencing of people, places, and historical topics.

A.R. Burn, *Persia and the Greeks: the Defense of the West, c. 546–478 B.C.* New York: St. Martin's, 1962. Burn's book is considered by historians to be the best study of the Persian invasion of Greece. Burn documents his conclusion well and provides interesting insights into Herodotus's history.

Diodorus Siculus, *Library of History*. Trans. C.H. Oldfather. Vol. 2. Cambridge, MA: Loeb Classical Library, 1954. Diodorus Siculus, a first-century B.C. Greek historian, recorded the early history of the Middle East by reading earlier writers and summarizing their works. Although not considered one of the great ancient historians, his work does fill gaps not covered by earlier writers.

Richard Frye, *The Heritage of Persia*. Cleveland: World, 1963. Frye's history covers the four-thousand-year history of Persia. The first chapters cover the history of the Persian Empire and it is well documented with archaeological discoveries and photographs of Persian art.

Herodotus, *Persian Wars*. Trans. George Rawlinson. New York: Modern Library, 1942. Herodotus's great history covers two large topics: the Persian invasion of Greece and Herodotus's travels to Persia and Egypt. Herodotus is considered the first great Greek historian and is acclaimed by modern historians for his great work, although they note his pro-Greek bias and exaggerations.

Tom B. Jones, *Ancient Civilization*. Chicago: Rand McNally, 1960. This book documents several empires, from the Persian through the Roman. Jones analyzes several in detail and draws general conclusions that characterize all of the empires.

A.T. Olmstead, *History of the Persian Empire*. Chicago: University of Chicago Press, 1948. Until Peter Briant's recent book on the Persian Empire, Olmstead's was considered the finest work on the empire. Although now dated and missing recent valuable archaeological discoveries, the book is still a solid study on the Persian Empire.

Strabo, *Geography of Strabo*. Trans. H.L. Jones. Cambridge, MA: Loeb Classical Library, 1954. Strabo, a first-century B.C. Greek geographer, traveled throughout the Middle East, Egypt, and those parts of Europe discovered by the Greeks. Although many of his writings are lost, he provides several geographical and cultural insights into the land and peoples he observed.

Joseph Wiesehofer, *Ancient Persia*. Trans. Azizeh Azodi. London: I.B. Tauris, 1996. Wiesehofer provides a series of essays on a variety of Persian Empire topics from customs and art to religion and royalty.

Xenophon, *Anabasis*. Trans. Carleton L. Brownson. Cambridge, MA: Harvard University Press, 1961. The *Anabasis*, also called *The March Inland*, is his story of the march of ten thousand Greek mercenaries into Persia to aid Cyrus III, their battles, and their ensuing return to Greece. Xenophon provides vivid descriptions of Persian peoples and customs.

———, *Cyrus*. Trans. H.G. Dakyns. London: J.M. Dent & Sons, 1914. Also sometimes called *The Education of Cyrus*, Xenophon writes a book about Cyrus III and why he was a great historical figure. Xenophon openly reveals his admiration for the Persian general and discusses Cyrus's qualities and the education that made him a great leader.

———, *Hellenica*. Trans. Carleton L. Brownson. Cambridge, MA: Harvard University Press, 1968. Xenophon wrote this book about the politics of Greece during the end of the fifth century B.C. Xenophon expresses many personal views of the politics of the leading Greek city-states.

Internet Sources

Eye Witness to History, "Alexander Defeats the Persians, 331 B.C.," 2000. www.eyewitnesstohistory.com/alexander.htm.

Farsinet, "Cyrus Charter of Human Rights Cylinder," www. farsinet. com/cyrus.

George Grote, "Conquests of Cyrus the Great," *History World International*. http://history-world.org/persians2.htm.

INDEX

PICTURE CREDITS

ABOUT THE AUTHOR

James Barter received his undergraduate degree in history and classics at the University of California in Berkeley followed by his graduate degree in ancient history and archaeology at the University of Pennsylvania. Mr. Barter has taught history as well as Latin and Greek.

A Fulbright scholar at the American Academy in Rome, Mr. Barter worked on archaeological sites in and around the city as well as Etruscan sites north of Rome and Roman sites in the Naples area. Mr. Barter also has worked and traveled extensively in Greece.

Mr. Barter resides in Rancho Santa Fe, California, and lectures throughout the San Diego area.